Advance P █████████

"With the new book, Joyce has skillfully drawn on her personal experiences as both a mother and an entrepreneur to document the stories of a new breed of 'Millionaire Mom.' Through a series of very engaging autobiographical essays written by women who have run the gamut of entrepreneurial successes—and failures—Joyce generously imparts to her reader one of most valuable lessons that we as entrepreneurs must all accept to survive: You learn from experience. And you must never stop learning. Great read!"

Fran Tarkenton, Founder & CEO, Tarkenton Companies
NFL Hall of Fame, Minnesota Vikings & NY Giants

"Millionaire Moms is dedicated to helping all women achieve their dreams. Joyce Bone is passionate about helping you find your inner hero!"

Chilli Thomas
Grammy-Winning Singer, Actress & Entrepreneur

"This book is uplifting, inspiring and full of wonderful ideas and insights to enable you to realize more and more of your true potential - in every area."

Brian Tracy, Author, *The Way to Wealth*
Personal Development Expert

"Joyce Bone has extracted the essence of how to succeed in life and business for the women of today. All Millionaire Moms-to-be will laugh and cry and ultimately benefit from the combined wisdom of these honest and inspiring success stories."

Rebecca Matthias, Founder & President
Destination Maternity Corporation
World's Largest Maternity Clothes Apparel Retailer

"Joyce Bone shares the wisdom of her personal journey and the life-lessons learned by other millionaire moms who have found their passion and built dynamic businesses. This book can open doors for every entrepreneurial woman."

Monica Smiley, Editor & Publisher
Enterprising Women Magazine

"Joyce Bone is a wonderful example for Mom's who want to build a successful business while creating an amazing family life. This book brings valuable insights and techniques to support women in this journey. It is a "must read" for all Mom-preneurs."

Nicki Keohohou
CEO of the Direct Selling Women's Alliance

Millionaire Moms

The Art of Raising a Business & a Family at the Same Time

JOYCE BONE

New York

Millionaire Moms™

The Art of Raising a Business & a Family at the Same Time™

Copyright © 2010 Joyce Bone. All rights reserved.

ISBN 978-1-60037-692-4

Library of Congress Control Number: 2009934413

Edited by Lorraine E. Fisher
Off Ramp Publishing
www.OffRampPublishing.com
San Diego, CA

MORGAN · JAMES
THE ENTREPRENEURIAL PUBLISHER

Morgan James Publishing, LLC
1225 Franklin Ave., STE 325
Garden City, NY 11530-1693
Toll Free 800-485-4943
www.MorganJamesPublishing.com

Games by Deborah Thomas
SillyMonkey International
www.sillymonkeyinternational.com
Atlanta, GA 30319

Cover background photo by Mary Buck
Lightscapes Photographic Artwork
www.lightscapesphoto.com
Duluth, GA.

In an effort to support local communities, raise awareness and funds, Morgan James Publishing donates one percent of all book sales for the life of each book to Habitat for Humanity. Get involved today, visit **www.HelpHabitatForHumanity.org**.

Dedication &
Acknowledgements

God in humble gratitude for all my blessings.

Alan for his unconditional love, support, loyalty, friendship and belief in me.

Griffin, Alex & Ethan – There is no greater love than the love of a mother for her children. You are my reasons "Why." I am so proud of each of you and blessed to be your mom.

Mom & Dad for the example of faith, love and commitment you established for your children. I couldn't have asked for better parents. You are my heroes!

Jeanine for providing me with ample opportunities for emotional IQ growth and in the end, always looking out for me. Jim, Megan, Kathryn, Emily & Allison—I love you all so much!

Joe, for the valuable lessons. We miss you so much.

John, for always being up for fun. I couldn't have asked for a better little brother. Nastia & Gabriella for bringing happiness to our family.

Jenny for being our "shiny penny." You are such a good person. Jay, for being our favorite Canadian!

Jessica, I love your intelligence and vulnerability. You make us proud!

Coach Crockett & Coach Poulos, my high school basketball coaches. You're the best! Thanks for all your encouragement, time, accountability and laughs. You made a difference in my life.

Raymond & Karen Cash. For your faith in me. I wouldn't be who I am today without you-much love & gratitude.

To my friends & supporters of Millionaire Moms. Thank you all for making this a fun journey. I appreciate you all so much! Lorie Marrero, thanks for being my accountability partner and being a great friend. Yesenia Leonard, thanks for being my cheerleader. Susan Wranik for your keen insights. Bonnie Bailey, for your editorial coaching and perfectionist's eye for details. Robyn Spizman & Tory Johnson for suggesting I do this in the first place. Deborah Thomas, for being my favorite "silly monkey." Lorraine Fisher, for being brave & fighting through your challenges to edit this book. Debbie VanGaale, for your wisdom and light. I am truly blessed to call you my lifelong best friend. You are my sister by choice. Jenifer, my MBA buddy. It was an enlightening adventure. "The Hofer" my favorite professor. Brian Bartes, for being a great friend and supporter. Stevie Puckett, for everything!

Special thanks to the millionaire moms and experts who contributed to this book. Your willingness to share your journey is much appreciated.

To all the moms, entrepreneurs and readers, your efforts matter! Keep up the good work. Keep going!

Foreword

Women are the most amazing creatures on the planet. We do it all, from nursing our children to supporting our families, to running corporations to inspiring generations. Our responsibilities are great, but we rise to the occasion again and again. As a mom, entrepreneur and one third of the Grammy and American Music Award-winning group TLC, I know all about wearing numerous hats to say the least. The good news is that women are natural multi-taskers and excel at reinventing themselves at the drop of a hat. I am a mom, a singer, a dancer, an actress, and entrepreneur all at the same time and I love it!

Women who run their own businesses are setting an amazing example for their children. They, in turn, often follow in mom's footsteps to become contributing, independent members of society. To me that is the best reward of all. It's important for my son Tron to see me as a loving, independent and, yes, successful woman! As parents, it's crucial to lead by example; as my son watches me it's only natural that he learns to mimic that behavior. I want him to have that drive and one day seek a mate with the same ambition. This book does an excellent job of showing how other moms have successfully combined their unpaid work–raising their children–with their chosen work, raising their business.

I have been asked why it was so important for me to branch off and start my line of purses, handbags and totes: Bagsbychilli.com. Yes,

I was blessed to have a great career, but there's so much more to me. And there is so much more in you! Let's face it, everything in this life is expensive. Life throws us unexpected curve balls. It's imperative to have money coming in from all different avenues. It only makes sense to have as many streams of income as possible. What better way to make that happen than by owning your own business?

Our life's work is seldom clear cut. We learn as we take action and as our personal lives evolve. Tomorrow is not promised. Today is a gift. By being clear on what is important, I have been blessed with an amazing and satisfying career. I believe you can be too! Yes, Ladies, we can have our cake and eat it too!

My friend Joyce is dedicated to helping all women achieve their dreams. She is passionate about helping you find your inner hero! Having been the underdog herself, she truly believes you can reach for the stars and grab hold of them. The other millionaire moms within are living proof of what is possible if you only believe. She covers the topics of importance in making your entrepreneurial dreams a reality. This book is for women who want to shine in business and in life.

Chilli Thomas
Grammy-Winning Singer, Actress, Dancer & Entrepreneur

Table of Contents

TREASURE HUNT ON THE MILLIONAIRE MOMS WEBSITE

If you're serious about earning an income while raising a family, then try this treasure hunt. Go to the website http://www.millionairemoms.com and join for free!

Once you sign up you will receive a confirmation email that will include a secret code for you. It is a slogan that is the last sentence of the welcome email. When you decipher the code, you will simply send Joyce a message to let her know that you got it. You will receive a free 20 minute coaching session with Joyce. You can send Joyce the code at support@millionairemoms.com or send the code message via:

Twitter: http://www.twitter.com/millionairemoms

Facebook: http://www.facebook.com/joycegrimesbone

LinkedIn: http://www.linkedin.com/in/joycebone

CHAPTER ONE

Who Is Joyce Bone?

Nature vs. Nurture

As the founder of MillionaireMoms.com, I am often asked to speak to groups. Those in the audience typically want to know, "How'd you do that?" in response to hearing how I grew a company so quickly and took it public. After all, I was a stay at home mom with very limited resources. People want to know what the formula for success is. To answer that question, I am going to tell you the whole story. I think it will shed light in a way that a sound-bite, 30-minute speech never could. Thank you for taking an interest in this book and my life. After reading my story, I hope you will see "life happens." There is no one who escapes unscathed, but in the end, that's ok. What we struggle with ultimately adds to the richness and quality of life's tapestry. My message to you is be strong, believe in yourself and make things happen! I believe we are products of our environment rather than beings predestined by genetics. The great news is that environments can be changed and results altered. My goal is to empower you to have the confidence to go after your dreams! It is time for everyone to be valued for what they can contribute instead of stereotyped and dismissed. All it takes is belief in oneself and creating a network of support along the way. That is the purpose of Millionaire Moms: to have a landing pad for everyone to get together, because great ideas spread.

I come from an Irish-Catholic family of eight. I had a mom and dad, three sisters and two brothers. My dad was born into a family with eight kids. He had a tough but loving upbringing and raised us the same way. He was "the word" in our house. I'd describe him as a loving but strict task master. It was made clear early on there would be no free rides in our house. There was no room for laziness. It was out of bed early, off to school and then work. I remember falling asleep in class often. I went to school, played varsity basketball after class, then would head off for a shift as a waitress until 11 p.m. or later, then homework when I got home. I paid the price during the day.

My math teacher, Mr. Hobbs, was a lovely old Southern gentleman. His class happened to fall right after lunch. His room had no air-conditioning. I sat next to the window. The Georgia sun would warm my skin, and I often dozed. I fell asleep every day in his class. Instead of admonishing or ridiculing me, he'd gently shake my shoulder and say, "Wake up Sleeping Beauty. It's time for you to learn some math." I would wake up to see his face smiling down on mine. My math angel. I have been blessed with loving role models in my life: loving parents, teachers and my coaches.

My father insisted I learn how to change the oil in the car and change a tire. I remember painting the outside of the house with him. I used to complain, arguing I'd have boyfriends and a husband to do this work for me. He wanted his daughters to be independent. The day before I got married he asked me to scrub down the outside of the house with bleach. I said, "No way! I'll ruin my nails and it will get in my hair!" His response? "Fine, if you don't want the house to look nice then don't do it." I have always adored him in spite of his hard driving ways. I remember being three years old trying to decide if I should marry my dad or my dog when I grew up. I certainly inherited my father's work-horse nature.

My mom had it tough growing up. Her answer was to join a convent for five years. She was three months away from being ordained a nun when she changed her mind. She felt the nuns lived "too high on the hog." She is the least materialistic person I've ever met. Her rock is her relationship with Jesus. She decided she wanted to have a big family and raise them in a loving home. She accomplished her goal. It hasn't always been pretty, but we've stuck together through thick and thin.

She was the opposite of my dad. She couldn't do enough for us. We could do no wrong in her eyes. I remember I backed into a car a week after getting my license. I gave the lady my insurance information. I was too afraid to tell my parents, so I didn't. That night at dinner the phone rang. My stomach fell to the floor. I heard her saying, "Oh, no, this must be a mistake...my daughter would NEVER back into a Mercedes." She'd defend us to the death.

Another time I did something dumb and said, "I am so stupid!!" My mother got upset and said, "You are NOT stupid. You are smart. Take it back!" We proceeded to have an argument as to whether I was smart or stupid. I argued that what I had done was dumb. She maintained I was smart. We went back and forth until I thought about the situation and started laughing. I decided to let her win that one! I liked her side of the argument better.

Dad lost his job in the early 80's. This was the first taste of downsizing, and at the time we had no idea it was the start of a trend. Things got tough. We had no heat in the house. I used to get dressed in front of the kitchen oven because it was so cold everywhere else. Our TV broke and we went without one for a year. There were no funds to fix it, so we all got used to reading books. We did, however, ride to church on Sundays in a limo! That's right, a limo. One of my dad's temporary jobs while looking for long-term work was as a limo driver. I thought that was big fun!

Rooting for the Underdog

I think of myself as an even-tempered person unless someone backs me into a corner or attacks my family or friends. I always stick up for the underdog and cannot tolerate bullies.

In kindergarten I got sent to the principal's office for beating up a third grader. My older sister was getting her butt kicked by this girl on the way home from school. She was sitting on top of her, pounding her face in. I warned her to get off, but she didn't listen. I guess she was having too much fun wailing on my sister. I felled her with one swift knock to the head with my Raggedy Ann & Andy lunch box. They were made with metal in those days. She ran home crying. Of course, we didn't say a word about it at home. I was sent to the principal's office the next morning. He had a soft spot for me. I told him my side of the story. He just winked and with a smile told me not to beat up the older kids anymore.

The next year, another kid was picking on my older brother, so I laid in wait in the bushes for him with my sister. As he rode by on his bicycle, I took a big stick and plunged it into the spokes of his front wheel. The bike completely stopped and he went flying. I called him a nasty name and told him to stay away from my brother (or else!). We got in big trouble for that one!

My career as a little stinker didn't stop there. I had a really mean third-grade teacher who used to hit us with a xylophone stick. My mom gave me some candy to give her for Christmas. I had a pet goose named Gary. I decided to exchange her gift of candy for an envelope full of goose poop. I ate the candy walking to school that morning, then placed the wet envelope full of goose crap on her desk. I got away with it, and to this day it still makes me smile!

As I grew, I stopped being physical with people. This doesn't mean, however, that I back down from a bully when challenged. When I ran EarthCare–the company we took public–I quickly found out there were some industry practices that were, in my opinion, unethical. Our corporate protocol was to correct the inconsistencies immediately upon purchase, which we did.

I had a competitor who knew what the industry practices and standards were but wasn't aware that we had policies in place to correct the situation. He set up a meeting with me and my Operations guy. I thought it was a "friendly" meeting to see if we could create synergies and develop a relationship.

Instead, he sat across from me and threatened if we didn't use his services he would "expose" me to the media. I couldn't believe it! He was threatening me. I stood up, leaned across his desk and got right up close to his face said, "Screw you, A___hole. Bring it on!" turned on my heels and walked out. My Operations guy was dying laughing and said, "Dang woman. I didn't know you had that in you! That was awesome!"

I have other stories of people trying to push me around in business and in life. The point is, don't let anyone do that to you. A bully is a bully no matter what the situation. The only way to deal with them is head on. If you call them out into the light, they quickly deflate and go scurrying back to the shadows.

A Desire to Succeed

Reminiscing again on my youth, my drive to be financially independent reaches all the way back to the seventh-grade field trip to Washington, D.C. All my friends got to go. I wanted to go very badly but pretended I didn't because of the money and my parents' situation. I watched my friends climb on board the big bus with their pillows, all excited about the upcoming adventure. My father let us know that money didn't grow on trees. "No" seemed to be his favorite word. Eventually, I knew the answer before I asked it, so I stopped asking.

I was a very good athlete, but it was rare for anyone to show up to watch. It never really bothered me. I played sports for the sheer love of the game. As an adult I realize how important it is for children to see that their parents are interested in their lives. By attending their events, parents speak volumes. By not attending their events, we still speak volumes.

If I wanted something I knew if it was meant to be it was up to me! I bought my first car at 16 years old for $300.00. A chocolate brown 1974 Buick LaSabre—big as a city block. It was a proud moment I shared with my younger brother. We went joyriding all over our hometown. The car stopped about two hours later. We sat there scratching our heads. I just knew I had been ripped off! A man pulled over to help us. He asked, "What happened?" I said, "I don't know. It just stopped." He sniffed around a bit and said, "Your problem is you are out of gas." "Oh." It was here that I learned owning material possessions creates ancillary expenses…like gas! That put a quick end to our joyriding ways.

I surrounded myself with friends and was overall a happy kid. I'm naturally optimistic. I do remember feeling like a loner even in the middle of a group of friends. That might have been teenage angst or it might have been I felt different because my friends were carefree with little responsibilities to be concerned with. As the middle kid I ducked attention at home, preferring to do my own thing with friends. As a result, I've made some big mistakes (and continue to make them), but overall I'm satisfied that more good decisions than bad have been made to date.

College Coed

I ended up attending three different colleges before graduating from one of them. I didn't even bother applying until my friends started leaving for their universities late in the summer after our senior year of high school. I figured I might as well go too. I was almost stopped before I started when I was asked to produce immunization records. I knew I had it done. I recalled the shots hurting. Tracking down the records, however, was going to be a major headache. I read the school's policy on it. I caught a little loophole that said, "Christian Scientist exempt from submitting records." I converted on the spot and got out of tracking down records. I've always struggled following rules except those I made myself!

I spent a year at my first school and decided it was time to move on. I told my guidance counselor I was going to "Dayton." I grew up in the South. I tend to drop letters off the end of words. I guess this translated to "Datin'." He said, "Excuse me for sticking my nose in where it might not belong but I would imagine a pretty and intelligent girl like you could go on dates and attend college at the same time." I started laughing. I replied, "That would be University of Dayton."

I left with a student loan and $30 for gas to Dayton, Ohio and nothing else. I had no food budget, no cute dorm accessories, nothing. My carefully laid plan had backfired. For my high school graduation my dad had bought me a car for which I was supposed to pay him back. Fifteen months later I hadn't. My game plan had been to sell the car and use the funds to pay for my food, books and entertainment needs at school. It all worked perfectly. I sold the car right before I left. That morning I asked for the check. My dad said, "What check?" I knew there was trouble with his opening statement. I also knew my father. I was out of luck. He wasn't going to back down.

I walked out of the house miffed. I managed to hit my head on a bee's nest in the magnolia tree next to the driveway and get stung a few times. I hopped into the car and said, "Let's get out of here!" I watched my mom wave goodbye, happy to be free at last!

Fast forward a few hours and I was now an Ohio resident. I got a job as a bartender that same day. My cousin went to school there too. He couldn't believe I landed one of the coveted college bartending jobs two hours after arriving in town. He said he applied there every year for three years. He wanted to know how I did it. I said, "Well, I had my tank top and shorts on. I walked in and asked "Are y'all hiring?" They asked if I could start the following afternoon at 4 p.m. That pretty much did it. Mystery solved.

Friends used to sneak me sandwiches and that's how I ate...that and ramen noodles. Yuck! Bartending took care of the social side and afforded book money so I was set. I did wish I had a meal plan but never dwelled on it. I was happy to be free!

My roommate came from one of those "Ozzie & Harriett" families. She had framed pictures of her family smiling on vacation in some fabulous destination. I remember looking at the photos wistfully. I decided that's how my family would be when I started my own.

Seeing the Future

The same weekend I sold my car was the weekend I met my future husband. It was 30 days before I left for Ohio. He is five years older than I. At that point, I was a girl and he was "a man." I never thought it would last when I left for school. I was raised to be realistic. He was a grown man with a life. I was a coed leaving for a school eight hours away. This was pre-email when you didn't call anyone until after 11 p.m. when the rates dropped.

I told him to date other people and I'd see him at Christmas. He didn't like that so much. He made me choose him or the other guys on the spot. I liked his moxy. He was the first guy to draw a line in the sand and stand up to me. He really was a man. He knew what he wanted and he wasn't playing games.

I thought it would fizzle out but agreed to his terms. He knew I would float away given my earlier comments and social nature. He made it a point to put his face in front of mine every two weeks. He drove 16 hours round trip twice a month for the entire year so I wouldn't give up on us. I ended up transferring back to Kennesaw State University in Georgia to spare him all that travel. There is a business lesson here … to quote Sandra Yancey from eWomenNetwork, "Put your face in the place and be seen on scene" if you want to make things happen or close a deal. Otherwise, you will be forgotten.

I say my husband "picked me" and that was that. He was there for me in the early years. When I returned from college I needed a car. My priest at church had one for sale for $2,000. I had to get a loan, and my dad refused to cosign. Alan cosigned for me even though we were only dating at the time. We have walked the same road for more than half my life now. We have been through a lot together, both happy and hurtful. His belief in me and loyalty to me have never wavered. I'm not the easiest person in the world to be married to. But then again, neither is he! That's a long-term marriage though. Forgive and forget and be mindful of each other's core needs. We learned that the hard way, but better late than never! I think people who put their faith in a higher power as front and center instead of themselves fare better in life and marriage. I'm still working on that.

I ended up renting a three bedroom house by myself, paying for college and my car. I paid off the University of Dayton school loan from my year away. I paid for my wedding. I never relied on the traditional support system of family. I was quite independent. Life was easy breezy. We were young and in love. It was a good time of life.

(Raymond) Cash is King

My first exposure to a successful entrepreneur came as a result of a modeling job. I met my mentor, Raymond Cash, at a fundraiser at which I was hired to work.

We hit it off, and I ended up working full time for him during the day while attending college full time at night. This intense schedule taught me the power of focus. I went from earning average grades to getting straight A's my last two years because I was forced to apply myself due to time constraints.

I watched Raymond build and sell three businesses and make a fortune doing it. He'd build then sell to national consolidators. It is this business model we ultimately replicated in a different, yet similar, industry.

Raymond would share little pearls of wisdoms with me saying things like "You'll never get rich working for someone else," "Live below your means so you always have options," "Pigs get fat and hogs get slaughtered" (this means don't be greedy in a deal), "He's all hat and no cattle" (referring to flashy people). Sometimes I'd sit across from him in his office waiting for him to get off the phone. I'd watch him "doodle." He was always scribbling something while on the phone.

Sometimes he'd scribble a "10" on a piece of paper and hand it to me (indicating he thought I was a 10). He really believed in me and took me under his wing. Don't get me wrong. He expected loyalty and hard work from everyone who worked for him. I worked hard for him. During the two years I went to school full time I never had a day off. The company policy was zero vacation for the first two years. After two years you got one week. He was definitely "the boss." The buck stopped with him.

The third time he sold his company, I ended up going with the new company as he was retiring. It became evident quickly they didn't see me as a "10" like Raymond did. It was a typical corporate environment in a male-dominated business. Women were only good for receptionist positions or as salespeople. I was in sales. After I trained my fifth boss to be the boss of me I thought, "This is crazy. Why can't *I* be the boss of me??" I knew I had to make a change.

And Baby Makes Three

The change came in the form of a bouncing 10 lb. 9 oz. baby boy named Griffin. My husband and I decided I should be a stay-at-home mom.

I figured trading in my non-expanding corporate career was a good move. After all, how hard could taking care of a baby be? Little did I know! It was a horrendous first year for me. My son nearly died at birth. His APGAR score (the health rating they give all babies that ranges from 1 to 10, with 10 being healthiest) was a 2. He was 12 days late and too big.

After 15 hours of contractions every two minutes (which is what happens when you are induced) with my baby's head already out, I was told they were going to have to push him back in and do an emergency C-section. I had a nurse literally sitting on top of my chest with her bottom in my face trying to push him out of me. He was in respiratory distress. They broke his collarbone to get him out. It was like giving birth to a watermelon! He was rushed to the NICU with severe meconium aspiration pneumonia, which, although rare, left him completely deaf in one ear.

It was like a scene out of the TV show "ER." They grabbed him, and everyone ran out of the room. It went from about 10 people in the room to just me. I had sent my husband with the baby so I was completely alone. I lay there—battered, bruised and swollen. My sister, who is a nurse, finally came into the room and was livid that they left me in that condition. Griffin and I were both in the hospital for a week. Welcome to the joys of motherhood!

The fun didn't stop there. He breastfed every two hours for six months. This meant I went six months without more than two hours of sleep at a time. I nearly died of exhaustion. I didn't recognize it at the time, but I had postpartum depression or some type of anxiety disorder. The first time he slept four hours I nearly wept with happiness.

It had been physically brutal on me starting at the time of his delivery. I remember being scared as hell as they pushed me out the hospital doors in a wheelchair with the baby. He had an IV sticking out of his head. I had never felt so vulnerable in my life.

My husband was thrilled! He was so happy. I sat in the back with the baby, feeling terrified and sick to my stomach. By the time we pulled in the driveway I was a complete emotional mess. My neighbor was outside mowing his lawn. He stopped and came over to see us as we pulled in. My husband rolled down the window so he could see. He commented on the baby and asked how I was doing? I burst into tears. The two men looked at each other and didn't know what to make of me. My neighbor quickly went back to mowing his lawn!

The Boardroom or the Playroom

It turns out trading in the corporate job for the mommy gig wasn't the cake walk I expected. I used to get jealous watching the 6 a.m. news reports of the people stuck in traffic. I'd be sitting there breastfeeding my son and think, "Lucky bastards, stuck in traffic after a full night's sleep. I bet they're sitting there sipping coffee, having the time of their lives!" The lack of sleep was really messing with me.

In hindsight, it was really dumb of me to put myself through that. I should have started feeding my baby formula and asked for help. I wanted to be the best mom ever no matter what sacrifices it took. My mom sacrificed freely for her children. Wasn't this what was expected of me? This is typical of women ...do what is expected no matter what the cost. Do what we "should" do.

My son's birth experience had left him disadvantaged health-wise. He had constant ear infections, RSV, asthma; you name it, he got it. He'd scream and cry any time we put him in the car seat. I remember my sister giving me grief for not driving 45 minutes to see her. After all, I had the time as a stay-at-home mom.

She came over one day and we took Griffin for one of his check-ups. The entire time he was in the car he screamed. She looked at me and said one word, "Wow." I started living my life in a bubble, afraid of germs, afraid to go anywhere he might cry or be exposed to more trauma. The other moms must have thought I was nuts, but his delivery had left him vulnerable. I was going to protect him.

The good news is that he is now a healthy, strapping teenage boy. He is a gifted athlete and a wonderful person. One of my proudest moments happened recently. He received the Leadership Award for his middle school. That speaks volumes. I know he is on the right track. Griffin is a great kid. I'm proud he's my son. As he enters his high-school years I have no doubt he will continue to excel. All those sleepless, worried nights were so worth it!

The Mommy Fog Lifts

As he got older, I regained the ability to process a thought. Once I started thinking again, it became obvious to me that we were short on cash. Having gone from two incomes to one had cobbled our discretionary funds. So here I was, 27 years old with a baby with tentative health, no money, no date nights, no shopping other than the basics. Life was becoming very gray.

I hit bottom standing in a Wal-Mart cleaning supply aisle. We needed more laundry detergent. I did the math calculations in my head and realized I would be over the household monthly budget for cleaning supplies. There was more time in the budget than money.

I was done. I started raging in my mind about all the times I had heard "No." I thought "I am sick and tired of "NO"!! I am tired of lack! Something has to be done. I don't want this life for my son or myself."

Remember the college photo of my roommate and her happy family vacations? That's what I wanted. I decided right then and there I was breaking this cycle and I would turn "No" into "How."

After my epiphany in Wal-Mart, I kept my eyes and ears open for opportunity. I ended up working one day a week for the lawyer who worked for my previous boss and mentor. It was here that I ran into a former co-worker. He mentioned how, after the acquisition had taken place, the overdue receivables had gotten out of hand. The man in charge of this was being transferred to corporate headquarters. The word on the street was he was sweating bullets about being held accountable for these unpaid invoices.

I drove home that afternoon and replayed the conversation in my head. I had done collections before. I was good at it, and it didn't bother me one bit to call people. This sounded like something I could do from the house if I had a computer. I had a plan worked out in my head by the time I pulled into the driveway. Immediately, I typed up a proposal and faxed it to him. I asked for the world. The reality was that I would have been happy with an hourly rate. He said, "Yes" without hesitation. I thought, "Yes to which part?" but he meant "Yes, to all of it." I was thrilled!

An Entrepreneur is Born

I set up shop in a spare bedroom. pcAnywhere afforded me access to the corporate computers at night in order to update accounts after everyone had left for the day. It worked beautifully. I was really happy. In six months I was on track to double the income I had made working full time prior to having a baby. This time, however, I was working six hours a week while my baby slept peacefully in his crib. I was hooked on entrepreneurship. I started thinking, "I'm really happy working. I'm making good money working six hours a week. I wonder what would happen if I did something full time?"

My husband traveled extensively at that time, which I didn't like one bit. He would say, "I wish I could stay home with you and Griffin instead of traveling." He was the primary bread-winner and felt the pressure to perform as such.

I had a conversation with him during which I said, "Look at what I've done so far. What if I did something bigger and better? Then you wouldn't have to travel or have all the financial pressures." He reminded me of our deal not ever to put our son in day care. We compromised that if I could find a family member to watch him at our house, I could start a more time- consuming business. It was with these parameters that I put on my "bigger thinking cap" to discover the business that was going to change our lives.

During this time two important things happened. I found the book *Think & Grow Rich* at the library and began reading it. As the classic personal-empowerment book it was a tad dry, but the concepts were good. Tony Robbins' "30 days to Personal Power" infomercial was on TV. He seemed to have all the answers I was looking for. I *really* wanted those audio cassettes. But if a gallon of laundry detergent wasn't in the budget, the $250.00 price tag for his cassettes was way out of the question!

I decided this was the first test of the universe to see how serious I was in building my empire. I put my thinking cap on and told myself, "There is no "no" anymore; there is only "how." *How* are you going to get those tapes, Joyce?" I looked over the budget. We tithed exactly $250.00 a month at that time. I decided there was no harm in skipping a month's donation to our church in favor of buying those tapes.

The plan was to buy the tapes, listen to them once and donate them to the local library. That way everyone in the community could benefit from the knowledge. Besides, when I became successful, wouldn't the church make more money off of our tithing anyway? This is what I ended up doing. The library was thrilled to receive them.

Tony said to describe your ideal life. I thought, "I have it pretty good: a husband who loves me; the most adorable baby boy in the world; a new, beautiful home; health and extended family. But if it were my ideal life, I'd have more money." The follow-up to this was to write specifics. How much money did I want and by when? I said a million dollars by the time I was thirty years old.

The next step was to come up with a business that would deliver on my goals. I challenged myself to write three business ideas a day for 10 days. I did not edit my thoughts. I remember coming up with ideas like "create a pneumatic tube that shoots your mail from your mailbox into your house" (like what they do at the bank). At the end of the ten days I had thirty ideas. Problem was they all stunk! I put the pen down and got pensive. I knew it would come to me.

Back to the Drawing Board

The next week I had lunch with my former boss and mentor, Raymond. He asked what I was up to. I told him my new game plan and shared some of my silly ideas with him. We had a good chuckle. Then we started talking about old times in the office. It was in that conversation that the idea for EarthCare emerged.

I asked him, "What if we did what you did but this time buy companies instead of being bought? Wouldn't it be fun to create a publicly traded company? We could be the ones at the helm calling the shots." All businesspeople know that the brass ring of business is taking a company public. The ultimate success! This appealed to him.

We took out a napkin and starting sketching ideas. It was the proverbial cocktail-napkin business plan. We shook on it in the parking lot. I remember getting into my car thinking, "We might be onto something here!"

I spent the next six months researching the viability of consolidating the non-hazardous liquid waste industry and created a rough business plan. I did most of my research in my alma mater's library at Kennesaw State University. I also picked up the phone and called business owners in this arena and peppered them with questions.

Raymond, his wife, Karen, and I went to the Opryland Hotel for this industry's national conference. You could literally see it was a fragmented market. There were no national companies. It was a bunch of mom and pops walking around in matching shirts and jackets. It was here that we decided it was time to move forward and go for it! It was exciting! I was in business with the smartest man I knew.

The intention for our company, EarthCare, was to take it public on NASDAQ in short order. Remember, my goal was to be a millionaire by the time I was thirty. I had two years to make it a reality. It is really helpful to know what your intention is from the get-go. It guides your decision-making process.

On the surface, the idea seemed laughable to people in my circle. How could I, Joyce Bone, a stay-at-home mom with modest savings, be capable of taking a company public? I say laughable because I actually had a lawyer laugh in my face when I told him my plans. That made me mad! It became the rocket fuel for my success. No one can steal your dreams unless you give them the permission to.

In reality, the cold, hard facts were more in his favor than mine. But what he couldn't see and didn't know are my life experiences leading up to that moment. He was not aware of the internal fortitude I possess. The odds may have been stacked against me, but the myriad lessons I had learned in childhood had made me unstoppable. To him I was simply a stay-at-home mom. *Never underestimate the power of a Mom*! He didn't know that I already had my first investor lined up who believed in me 100 percent. I have always worked hard. I have always had a knack for figuring things out. The world is not going to cut you a break because *you* think it should. You must find a way to *demonstrate* through actions (not words) your capabilities. That's what I have done.

I have learned over the years that other people's opinions of me are really none of my business. I chose to be my own cheerleader instead of hoping for other people's approval. This, in turn, allowed me to make much better decisions. If you expect to be underestimated, it will make the victory that much sweeter when you do overcome the obstacles!

A Million (or 13) Ways to Succeed

Raymond offered $1 million cash, and I put in $10,000.00. That might not seem like much, but it was all I had. I was committed. We leveraged this into an additional $13-million-dollar line of credit. You may be thinking it was a stroke of luck that I found someone willing to put up a million dollars. Well, yeah, I'm lucky! But I *make* my luck—as we all do—by keeping my eyes open to opportunity, working hard and taking chances.

I committed to a journey and took consistent (unpaid) action with positive expectations. The universe seems to embrace people who do this. The right people seem to show up at just the right time. Closed doors open. Is this because of something mystical? Maybe. But perhaps it's that influencers sit up and take notice of passionate, driven, and committed people dedicated to doing big things. It's exciting to be around big thinkers! In this case it was me, but it could just as easily be you.

I was definitely blessed to have Raymond as a partner and friend. One of the reasons he was prepared to invest was that he knew my work ethic and understood the deal. He believed in me because I had proven myself worthy when I worked for him. Furthermore, I had skin in the game, too. The $10,000 was all the cash I had. Again, a tiny amount compared to a million dollars. But the relative risk was greater. It was everything I had. Raymond still had millions. I was 100 percent committed.

In addition, I was putting my "sweat equity" into the partnership, and in typical fashion I set out to conquer the world. It wasn't easy up front getting the owners of those small, liquid-waste businesses to take me seriously. But after they spent an hour with me, I had them convinced it was the best opportunity of their lives. *And it was.* The vast majority of those business owners made very nice livings but had no exit strategy. They were stuck with businesses that, if sold, were worth only a fraction of the lifestyle afforded them.

Growing the Business

Our first acquisition was a grease-trap business that we bought for $750,000 and named Bone Dry. We went to the bank with that asset on our books and leveraged it into a $13 million line of credit. Why $13 million? Because it's was Raymond's favorite number. I tell you this to show you how intuitive at lot of business decisions can be. When you look at business people and think they are somehow smarter than you, remember they're human, just like you, and might be taking a "WAG" (Wild Ass Guess) at the correct answer. The reason they stand out—and succeed—is because they take action anyway. They know that mistakes can usually be fixed or overcome.

My first day operating our new company, I had been in the building thirty seconds when an employee walked up and asked, "Are you new here?" I said, "Well, yes, I guess you could say I am." He said, "Great. We've needed extra help around here for a while." He then took a form out and said, "Could you make me 50 copies of this?" Our eyes locked. I processed his comment and then said, "I am more than happy to help you. Where is the copier?" I made him the copies. Thirty minutes later the whole company was gathered and I was introduced as the new owner. The look of shock registered on his face was priceless! He ended up being the first person I ever fired, but that's a different story.

Putting on my Big-Girl Pants

The business took off, and soon we needed more money to continue expanding. We raised approximately $13 million through a private-placement offering to some 50 wealthy individuals we knew from our industry. Aside from the time I brought my baby home from the hospital with tubes sticking out of his head, I have never been so scared!

Suddenly, there I was, talking numbers and "winging" my way through a high-stakes pitch to a room full of savvy businessmen! I did well enough on sheer adrenaline for us to get the money, but after that I joined Toastmasters and completed their Competent Toastmaster

(CTM) training. Never again did I want to be nervous taking the floor to convey my ideas.

Our next fund-raising move was to approach Bank of America, which agreed to give us a $40 million-dollar line of credit. I'll never forget that day. The stay-at-home mom gets a major bank to lend her $40 million dollars! No more lawyer-laughing soundtrack for me. I was the one laughing now.

Going Public

It wasn't long before we reached the $50 million mark in annual revenue and decided it was time to go public. That was in 1997, and IPOs were all the rage. "Initial public offering" is the term used to describe the first time a company issues shares of stock to the public.

All told, it took me 18 months to go from being a novice with the seed of a business idea to a significant stakeholder in a publicly-traded company listed on NASDAQ. EarthCare had grown from one employee—me—to 350, and from zero to $50 million in annual revenues, which ultimately reached $125 million.

I want to acknowledge here everyone who had a part in that success. This story may be what went on behind my eyeballs, but without the talent and efforts of our senior management team, the employees, and the owners who sold to us, it wouldn't have happened.

Clarity & Communication

If you don't know where you're going, then any road will lead you there. It is up to each of us to determine what we were born to do and then go after it. Start with the end in mind and identify your reasons for doing it. It's those *reasons* that will keep you going when you encounter the inevitable roadblocks and obstacles.

I am convinced that winning at the game of business takes more than being the smartest or the best educated. It's an individual's drive that counts. The person who takes action, stays focused on completing the (critical) task, and lives her life fully engaged—personally and professionally—is the true success story. The people I'm talking about constantly challenge themselves and go after what they want with zest.

To achieve your goals, what you have to do is be strategic, plot your course, and then take action in spite of not knowing all the answers. By committing 100 percent to your business, engaging in thoughtful, high-level activity every day, and infusing others with a sense of urgency, you will succeed.

As mysterious as it may seem, the process of going public is quite well-defined. It's not about knowing everything yourself, but about being able to tap into the appropriate resources: the right people who can make it happen.

The former CFO of EarthCare described the process as "little shovels to the mountain." Had we stopped to look at the mountain in front of us when we started, it would have seemed so daunting and complex we would have doubted our ability to accomplish the task at hand. But an IPO, or any sizable project for that matter, can be broken down into little pieces. You simply need to grab your shovel and get busy!

Hitting the Jackpot

I left the company at this point because we moved it to Texas. Remember the promise I made about no day care for our son? As part of my employee agreement, a clause had been written stating that if the company moved 50 miles outside of Atlanta, my salary would jump to the highest tier and I could opt to ride out my contract in Atlanta. This meant receiving six figures for two years for just walking to my mailbox. I missed out on the fun of participating in the road show, pitching Wall Street on our business, but overall, it was what was best for my family.

I had another baby. Life was perfection for a while. We had two beautiful boys. We were rich. We were young. My dreams had come true. Then, reality set in. My middle son's speech and behavioral problems started when he was two-and-a-half years old. He was diagnosed with several disorders. I spent the next three years taking him to three therapists a week for occupational therapy, behavioral and speech issues.

Again, I found myself staying in the house to protect my child. This time it wasn't health-related but behavioral. I didn't want him deemed "that kid" as in, "stay away from that kid!" He was very volatile during this time. I didn't want him tagged as a problem child. I just knew we could work him through it.

I will never forget when one counselor faced off with me and said, "Joyce, not everyone is as highly functioning as you are. Perhaps you need to adjust your expectations and let him be." I was livid. Here was my amazingly intelligent, beautiful child, and she was suggesting I let him wither on the vine? Forget that!

We worked hard, and he did get through it. It took seven years of speech therapy before he was finally cleared of all therapies. It was tough, but in the end so worth it. I have had moms call me after play dates and ask about my parenting style. How did we produce such an incredible child? What was the secret? Of course, I delight in those calls, but if they only knew what we went through to get there. Alex is incredible. He's a gifted writer and a well-mannered, considerate, funny, handsome, empathetic young man.

We discussed a third child. Should we? My husband wanted a third. We decided to have one more child. I became pregnant with naturally occurring triplets. I was shocked. I was even more shocked when I had a miscarriage at the end of my first trimester in the middle of my father-in-law's 70th birthday party. I drove myself home with a towel between my legs and dealt with it. I didn't want to ruin the party.

After a time, we became pregnant again with our third boy. Ethan has been a blessing since the day he arrived. Three definitely changes the dynamics and energy of a household! He is the only person in the world who has ever wrapped his arms around me, stared into my eyes with a smile and told me I was "enchanting." I'll bet you didn't know that about me! Basically, he has me wrapped around his finger with his humor and fun-loving attitude towards life.

After a two-year hiatus from EarthCare, I got involved in real estate. I did a bunch of different things . . . bought a 54-hole miniature golf course, managed rental properties, rehabbed houses. It was a good fit for our lives at that time with young children. It kept my mind busy and made money. The kids always rode along with me.

I remember my middle son wanted to skip preschool one day. I told him he'd have to go to work then. He said "fine." We rode out to a job site where I had about 10 people working. We hopped out of the truck. I gave a bunch of orders. We got back in and drove off. He said, "Mom, I thought we were going to work? Everyone was working but you!" I thought that was funny. I explained to him that I was the boss. I also explained in the entrepreneurial world the boss took the risk and got paid last (if at all). The risk and the reward fell on my shoulders. I'm not sure how much he retained of that, but he was insightful enough to pick up on the situation!

I saw that the market was shifting and sold off the real estate assets we didn't want to hold long-term. During this time, my older brother was diagnosed with cancer. It was in July that he called to tell us he was in the hospital and they were running tests. It turned out he had lung cancer.

The Biggest Loss

I thought he would beat it or they'd at least be able to extend his life. I visited him regularly. The day I realized he was going to die was December 14, 2007, my 40th birthday. I walked into the hospital room for a visit, and he had shrunk since I had last visited a few days earlier. Tears stung my eyes as my father and I exchanged knowing looks, but I kept a brave face on for my brother. I left early evening in order to attend my oldest son's basketball game. My sister pulled up next to me at a light and saw me crying. She knew why. A neighbor came up to me at the game to rib me about the fact that it was my birthday and my turning the big "4-0." I couldn't help myself. I burst into tears right there in the gym. It came to me in that moment that my brother's birthdays were over. It was embarrassing, and I felt bad for making her feel bad! I assured her it wasn't her fault.

My mother's birthday is January 6. We had a cousin die at age 14 of cancer on my mom's birthday. I reminded my brother of this. It was unspoken but understood that he shouldn't die until after her 70th Birthday. We had a big party trying to celebrate her in the midst of all this heartache. He had to stay in bed, but everyone got to visit with him.

The next day, a Monday, I sat with him and freaked out when I saw his feet had turned dark purple. We called the hospice worker, and she said it was a sign that death was near. I knew he would die on Wednesday. He asked me that day if I thought he was a "liver or a dier?" Cancer had spread to his brain by then. I told him, "Joe, you are a liver, of course!" My heart was breaking. Wednesday morning rolled around. I came with my family to be with him. My sons and husband said "Goodbye." They left and I stayed.

I settled in beside him. My parents, who had been by his side constantly, finally left to take care of their own needs. It was 10:15 a.m. Fifteen minutes went by and he was struggling to breathe. I put my arms around him and my head near his head. I leaned in and whispered in his ear that I loved him. He was a good brother to me. I said some prayers. I think it was more reassurance for me than him. I kept messing up the Hail Mary and the Our Father, although I know them by rote. I gave up praying since I was bungling it so bad and said, "Joe, you have suffered enough. It is ok to let go. I promise Mom and Dad will be looked after by all of us. They will be ok. Everyone has said their goodbyes. You can let go of the pain." The very next breath was his last. He just let go. Like that, he was gone. I was shocked. Was this really happening? I looked around the room to see if I could sense his spirit, but I couldn't. I thought, "I wonder if he's looking at me?" I was so sad sitting there alone with him. The hardest part was the knowledge that as soon as I walked through the doors my parents' world would be shattered forever. I stayed alone with him for a long while not wanting to devastate my parents but relieved his considerable pain had ended.

Finally, what had to be done was done. I called them in. It was horrible. My mother cried. My dad, who had always been tough on him, sat next to him and petted his lifeless hand. He was in his undershirt and underwear having just gotten out of the shower. My mother lost it. She was crying and calling his name over and over. My dad read the Shadow of Death passage from the bible out loud. My mother read a poem to him my 10-year-old had given her an hour earlier. She said it reminded her of him. Truly, it was the most horrible thing I have ever witnessed. I got up and called the funeral home. I handled the details of the arrangements. I wanted to spare my parents that pain.

Celebration of Life

I lost my mentor Raymond later that same year. Raymond died in December. I came across one of his "10's" recently in an old book. I put it in a tiny frame as a reminder of him and the faith he placed in me. He had such a profound effect on my life, and I miss his friendship. He was probably the most interesting person I've ever met. He was born in 1930 in Virginia and grew up in Georgia. As you can imagine, times were different then. You would expect someone of his generation to have prejudices, but not him. He valued people for their character and work ethic, not their gender or skin color.

At his funeral, I had to grin when I scanned the room. A lot of the attendees were older, African-American ladies in fancy church hats. The preacher was a "fire-and-brimstone" kind of guy, and this was his congregation. Raymond had donated the building these folks used as their church, and they were there to honor him.

The preacher relayed a story about how he went to Raymond, hat in hand, to make his request for the building. He told him he felt bad asking for a handout, but without this building, his church would have to disband. He'd be forced to go back to work in the secular world. Raymond's response was, "Son, you aren't asking for a handout. You are doing good work in the world. All you are asking for is a hand up." That was the quintessential Raymond.

No Guarantees

The sister of a high school friend of mine was recently murdered as a result of domestic violence. The friend knew my brother. I knew her sister. She told me when she saw her sister in the casket something snapped inside her. She made a vow to change the cycle she was in to honor her sister. She had dropped out of high school, married the wrong guy and was left holding the bag as a single mom. Since her sister's passing in the spring she has earned her GED and applied to college. One day at a time she is turning her world around.

The day after she buried her sister, my friend read these words: "The worst day of your life can be the most impactful if you chose it to be." I agree. Sometimes important people are ripped out of our lives. Change is thrust upon us whether we are willing participants or not. We are forced to grow or give in. It is how you choose to respond to the curves and jolts in life that determine destiny. There are no victims in life, only volunteers. It also serves as a daily reminder to appreciate and love those you hold near and dear.

My brother's death was the catalyst for me to write this book and share the story of empowerment via millionairemoms.com. It is my desire to reach out and encourage you to live your life to the fullest. The point is not money. It's about knowing what your ideal life looks like and setting out on the journey to create it.

Tomorrow is not guaranteed. I don't want you to have regrets when you get to the end of your life. Even if you fall on your face, at least you were brave enough to try. You took a swing at bat. Isn't that more rewarding in itself than wondering when it is too late, "What if?" God did not put you on this earth to be meek. Be a lioness! Take charge of your life.

Where is the joy in subordinating ourselves to the expectations of how others think we should live? Of giving up our precious time here on earth to live lives of quiet desperation? I, for one, plan to skid into my grave full blast all used up! A fulfilling life can be a painful struggle at times, but in the end it is so worth the effort. It really is. Remember:

Adversity facilitates growth. Adversity forces you to think at a higher level. Adversity allows you to start over more intelligently.

"What would you attempt to do if you knew you could not fail?"

Word Bank Puzzle

We think these are sayings that you should have in your memory bank—in other words, phrases that you should have on the ready! We have created this clever memory technique to help you file these sayings away safely in your memory word bank.

In each row there is a missing word. There is a clue at the beginning of the row that you can use to figure out the missing word. For instance, the missing word in row 1 has "mental image" as a clue. Use the clue to fill in the missing word in the 1ˢᵗ word column. And, yes, we provided some of the letters in the missing word to help you out, as well as the number of missing letters.

Instructions: Fill in the missing words. To help you get started we provided some of the letters and dashes that represent the number of missing letters in the word.

Clue	1ˢᵗ word	2ⁿᵈ word	3ʳᵈ word
Mental image	V_ s _ o_	provides	clarity
Lucidity	Cl _ _ i_ y	provides	confidence
Deed	Sureness	spurs	A_ t _ _ n
Victory	Action	spurs	S_ c _ e_ _

CHAPTER TWO

Motivation

*The truth about entrepreneurship is that it is
about seizing control of your own destiny.*

Margery Kraus, APCO Worldwide Founder

Why be an entrepreneur?

The answer, of course, is different for everyone. Every year, over eight million entrepreneurs start businesses in the United States alone. Each one of these businesses needs an energetic entrepreneur, a strong work ethic, and a great idea! Lots of moms cite flexibility of hours as their primary motive for choosing self-employment. They are willing to give it their all for compressed periods of time if they can keep their children the priority while adding to the family budget.

For some it's the appeal of being the one in charge—*being* "the (wo) man" instead of working for "the man." Those of us with a low tolerance for office politics and incompetent bosses may find this reason enough to consider starting our own businesses. For Christy Clarke, Founder of TableTopics, it was a family affair from the start. "I wanted our daughters to be involved in the business, and at the beginning they did all sorts of jobs for me: assembling press kits, stickering postcards, and sending samples. And for a while they ran the online store, pulling the orders off the web, charging the credit cards, and packing and shipping the boxes. They learned a lot about the business, and I loved having them involved. They went to China with me last year, which was an incredible experience for all of us. They visited the factories with me and sat in on the meetings I had with the manufacturers. We saw one of our containers being loaded, then spent an entire afternoon watching the cranes load containers onto ships bound for the U.S. Having them see a small business like mine up close, and know it's possible for them to do the same thing, is one of the incredible benefits we've all received from this business." What a fantastic gift she has given her daughters! Children model what they see, more than what they are told.

For many, cash is the motivation. Others start businesses as a means of creating employment, having been phased out of the corporate job market by age and/or level of experience. And as corporations continue to merge, "right-size" and go out of business, job uncertainty will steer more and more women toward entrepreneurial ventures in their quest for financial security. If you own your business, you are at least assured of being the last one fired.

There is also the motivational allure of fame, intellectual stimulation, or a sense of achievement. When you excel at what you do, people sit up and take notice. That's why successful entrepreneurs, as a group, are among the most interesting people you will ever meet. Whether they are known in only their local communities or recognized internationally, their fame is based on a reputation for business prowess, a quality with lasting power. Let's face it, a pretty face fades with time, but a keen and active mind stays with you until the end. As a consequence, successful entrepreneurs generally have healthy self-esteem. And why shouldn't they? They're winners, which is what we all strive to be!

Many women become entrepreneurs not so much because they want to, but because they *have* to in order to survive. Life circumstances have left them with no other viable choices. Statistics from the National Foundation for Women Business Owners indicate a woman's business motivations differ from a man's. Women want to be able to integrate family and business life, to utilize skills and passion, and are more open to seeking support, mentoring and interpersonal connections than men. The study revealed 38 percent name happiness and/or self fulfillment as the main driver, 30 percent the achievement and challenge of creating their own business, 20 percent to help others and 12 percent for profit. What's your reason?

Tony Robbins, the well-known motivational speaker, says, "Life will pay you any price you ask of it." Taking the time to get clear about what you want to achieve and then taking consistent, relentless action will produce amazing results in all areas of our lives! Seek and you shall find. Knock and the door will be opened.

It was important to me to be available for my son, which for me meant being in control of my time and calendar. In fact, it was becoming a mom that finally made me act on the impulse to become an entrepreneur. This is the case for the majority of the millionaire moms I interviewed. Raising another human being is a huge responsibility, and I knew I wanted to be present for my child. After eight years in the corporate world I also knew how *un*available a full-time job makes you for anything else. Sticking my son in daycare to continue working for someone else wasn't going to cut it.

If I had been older, I believe the "what ifs" would have reared their ugly heads and held me back. As it was, it never occurred to me that I would fail. Why would I?

Adversity and Survival

For some of the other millionaire moms I interviewed, adversity and the struggle for simple survival were what drove them to start their businesses. Ariana Reed, founder of Momswin.com, was only 17 and a single mom when she faced the cold, hard reality of having to be self-supporting with no real work experience or skills. When she asked herself, "What do I do well?" the answer at the time was "clean." So she literally picked up her cleaning products and her Oreck vacuum cleaner and launched a cleaning-services company as her first business.

Like Reed, Nadja Piatka falls into the category of women who became entrepreneurs to overcome adversity. A typical suburban mom, she saw her world turned upside down after her husband of 20 years came home and announced he no longer wanted to be married to her because he had found someone new. Almost overnight, she and her two young teenagers were uprooted from their big home and reduced to living in a small house on the wrong side of the tracks.

Nadja had not worked outside the home for decades and was caught totally off guard. Not only was she missing the skills to get a job, but the divorce and complete change of lifestyle had pretty much depleted her self-confidence. After one really bad interview (the only one she was able to get) she realized no one was going to hire her. This was a woman who had grown up with Ukrainian parents who owned a family business and always paid their bills. Now she was not only broke, but in debt. She recalls how bill collectors would come to the house and peer into the windows, walk around the house, and then knock on the doors and yell. "I would hide until they thought no one was at home and eventually leave," she says. "Unfortunately—or maybe fortunately, because this was a real turning point for me—the bill collector came when my daughter, Veronica, was home from school, and I made her hide under the table with me. It was the most humiliating experience to share that with her. We were on the floor on our hands and knees, nose to nose, and I made her stay under the table for 15 minutes. She kept saying, 'Mommy, I am going to be late for school. I've got to go.' I said, 'No, no, he is going to see us.'

"I was almost able to handle the bill collectors coming after me, but the day my daughter was there and heard him yelling at me, 'Deadbeat, I know you are in there,' was the turning point. The mother bear in me came out, and I was mad! I decided in that moment I was never, ever going to let anybody put me and my children in that position again. That situation made me determined to find every ounce of courage, talent and strength and make it work.

"The day my husband left, I had certain goals I had set out to accomplish. But the day of the bill collector's visit was the day I recorded them on the back of a pantyhose cardboard that was lying nearby. I wrote 'I will have a national business. I will be an author of a best-selling book (because in school my teacher once made a joke by telling me never to take a job in which I had to put two sentences together). I will have my own newspaper column. I will be a public speaker…I will have a TV show…I will bring value to people's lives.' And do you know, within a year most of those goals were achieved."

Fran Biderman-Gross was already involved in an entrepreneurial endeavor when adversity put her to the test. "It is amazing how your life can change in an instant. After my husband's death from cancer," she said, "I inherited all aspects of the company we had built together. Having no guidance, no mentor, no support, I had no idea how to succeed. I just knew I had to."

At the age of 20, Fran married her best friend of five years, David. Within less than a year, Fran learned she was pregnant, which derailed her plans to go to law school. In the meantime, David had finished college and was working for the family garment business. His vision was to be a millionaire by the time he was 30 and to do it "on his own" by creating a company with a culture that supported not only his desire to succeed but also allowed him to share the wealth with the "dream team" he would put together. When he realized the family business was not going to support his goals, he started, with nothing, a little company called Advantages. Soon it evolved in to a mom-and-pop printing business that revolutionized the industry by creating partnerships and essentially timesharing equipment.

"After about a year," Fran recalls, "he needed help managing the growth, and I started with the company to support him. We were a power team not to be reckoned with. Just as we were going to break our first $1 million in sales, the diagnosis came. Cancer. I had no choice but to take over running all aspects of the company. For two years, I lived my life in a blur. While David was being treated all over the world, even as far away as Germany, I would either be with him or with the kids, essentially traveling every Sunday. Week to week it changed.

I had three full-time jobs: researching David's illness, maintaining the business, and trying to keep our family from falling apart.

"After a two-year battle, I lost my husband, our kids lost their father, and Advantages lost its leader. I was left to carry on. Honestly, I am not sure how I got through each day. All I knew is that I would NOT fail. Skin my knees maybe, but NOT fail."

Statistically, the situations these three women faced are all too common among women in today's world. In her book *Rich Woman*, Kim Kiyosaki points out that 47 percent of women over the age of 50 are single. Women who marry run a 50 percent risk their marriages will end in divorce, resulting in an average drop of 74 percent in their standards of living the first year after divorce. Nearly seven out of 10 women will at some time live in poverty. Of the elderly living in poverty, three out of four are women. Eighty percent were not poor when their husbands were alive.

Changing Priorities

Julie Lenzer Kirk is an award-winning IT entrepreneur who after college worked for, in her words, a wonderful large company and loved what she was doing. The fact that she was also traveling about 70 percent of the time was not an issue. When she and her husband decided to start a family, her plan was to keep doing the same job and continue traveling. That was the plan anyway. Then after her daughter was born, Julie recalls, "Looking into those eyes, I just said, I can't raise a child from a hotel room. I had a very supportive husband who was willing to do whatever needed to be done, but it just wasn't what I wanted from my life. That's not why I became a mother.

"I looked at my options, actually interviewed with a lot of different companies, and I just kept coming back to this nagging thing in the back of my head that said, Why not start your own business? And it's funny, because when I finally did—when my daughter was six months old—the prevailing thought in my head was that if it didn't work out, I could always go out and get a 'real' job. ...Little did I know that it was going to be the most *real* job I ever had in my life. And once you become an entrepreneur, you often make a terrible employee for someone else."

Building a Better Mousetrap

Sometimes it's the desire to fix a problem or improve a situation that first leads millionaire moms to become entrepreneurs. Like Julie, Shelley Sun had a fairly "normal" career in corporate America when she and her husband became engaged in 2001. Then her husband's grandmother in Florida became very ill, and they were faced with the challenge of doing a remote search to find and hire a home-care company. Unfortunately, they lost his grandmother to cancer the day before they got married in early 2002. But, Shelley notes, "We looked to each other and said, 'Is this something that we could do better than what we were able to find, and are there other people like us who are looking for one-stop shopping as it relates to home care?' So that was the premise for BrightStar Health Care and how we got started in 2002—from a very personal experience—with home care services. We said, 'Let's build a company around providing continued care so that families really have an alternative to an assisted-living or a nursing home.'

According to Kayla Fioravanti, founder of Essential Wholesale natural and organic cosmetic bases, "What got me started, actually, was that my son had ringworm and we couldn't get rid of it. We had gone to the doctor, gotten three different prescriptions, and it just kept growing. So we went to the health food store, because I had kind of grown up doing that sort of thing: going to the health food store and looking for solutions. There all the books said to use tea-tree essential oil. I did, and after three applications the ringworm was totally gone. Before then I had thought aromatherapy was just a kind of "fru-fru" thing that didn't do anything. Also, I am allergic to chemicals and fragrance oils, so I had lived a scent-free existence my whole life, and because these were naturals from plants, they caused no allergy problems for me. I was absolutely sold, and we ended up starting a business around it."

What It Takes

> *"Success is almost totally dependent upon drive and persistence. The extra energy required to make another effort or try another approach is the secret of winning."*

Denis Waitley, American motivational speaker and author of self-help books

In a way, being entrepreneurial is about taking control of your life. One of the first questions you should ask yourself is: Is this going to be a "lifestyle" business or a growing, ongoing concern? By a lifestyle business, I mean one you create to bring in a little extra money to supplement your family budget: a part-time endeavor that will often take a back seat to your other commitments. My first company, for example, was a lifestyle business at which I worked six hours a week, dabbling at making money. By a growing, ongoing concern, like my second business, I mean a full-time commitment that absorbs your attention.

Next comes the chicken-or-the-egg question: Do I need to have the idea first before starting a business, or do I first decide to start a business and then look for an idea? In my opinion, it's more important to have made the decision and commitment to start your own business. My first company started with the idea. But for my second, even more successful venture, I made the decision first; the idea came later.

Once you've decided to be in business for yourself, it's time to replace any negative self-talk reels that may be playing in your head with plenty of positive pep talks. You must believe you are capable of pulling this off! You have to *believe* you have what it takes to be successful. It doesn't mean you know everything you need to know, or that you don't have shortcomings to contend with, but at the end of the day, you have to have the self-esteem required to gut it out.

Nancy Bogart, founder of Jordan Essentials, says to "trust your instincts." Having started her business after spending six years at home, with no computer skills and without ever having used a cell phone, she notes, "Too often in the early years I thought I was so inexperienced and that everyone else around me had better ideas and knew more; therefore, I often deferred the decision to them. I figured since I was *just* a mom, I must know relatively little. But it was my dream, and I took it one step at a time. Use your God-given strengths and be okay with learning new things without putting yourself down along the way. Be a life-long learner and enjoy the journey."

Start a business based on what you are passionate about so that you can wake up every day looking forward to going to work. As adults we spend the vast majority of our lives working. If you want a fulfilling life, you must have fulfilling work. Loving what you are doing and having a mission behind your goals makes all the difference when you are working your tenth straight 16-hour day. The passion and the mission provide the fuel to keep you going during the tough times.

Become a person of conviction and a decision-maker. Successful entrepreneurs take control of their lives. This means setting goals based on high expectations and then gearing up each day to achieve them. There is no room for "maybe." As Yoda from the *Star Wars* series says, "Do or do not;.there is no try." You must be 100 percent committed to your business success. According to data gathered by the Center for Women's Business Research, the more goal-orientated you are, the more likely you are to accelerate the growth of your venture.

At each new step in your company's growth, make a conscious decision to make it either a hobby-level business or a big business. Doing so helps you avoid getting stuck where you are by keeping your focus on the things that make you grow. It's really easy to get so busy working *in* your business that you don't spend any time working *on* your business. If you have made the decision to create a big business, it is critical that you focus on growth. In order to do that, you might have to work longer hours or hire someone to do some of the work. Oftentimes, business owners believe they are the only ones capable of doing all the aspects of their job well, but in reality, time freed up from some of the more administrative tasks propels their businesses forward.

Sandra Yancey, founder and CEO of eWomanNetwork, sums up what she perceives as the biggest issue with women: "We don't behave as CEOs, you know, Chief Executive Officers; we behave as COEs, Chief of Everything Officers. That, I think, is the recipe that will destroy you over time. It's kind of like the fly on the windowsill, trying to get out of the house. That raw determination, let me try a little bit harder, let me do it again, never give up. The next day you go back and the fly is dead. I mean, it's the epitome of what happens when you keep hitting your head up against the wall. So I think the real message is that you have got to stop the insanity - you have to slow down, and you have to understand that you can't do it by yourself. And you *shouldn't* do it by yourself. Because if you start a business and treat it like a job, where nobody else can do it but you, you really don't have a business; you have just that, a job. And you are working for a lunatic.

Another thing Sandra believes you need to do is surround yourself with other people who will support you, people you can inspire to see your vision for the business. If you're thinking that because you're not paying yourself; how will you be able to pay for somebody else to come in and help? Sandra's response is this, "The number-one way to start focusing on making the cash register ring is put your first person on the payroll, like I did. You know, I wasn't paying myself when I originally put Dale, my first employee who is still with me today, on the payroll. She said to me, 'I need you to know, Sandra, I love this, and I want to support you and I want to work for you, but this is a job. I need a paycheck every week, every Friday, and when you give me a check, I need to be able to cash it.' You should have seen what happened to me on Thursdays when I didn't have the money to pay Dale! I mean, I was working the phones; I was making the cash register ring. That really began to help me shift from the busy-ness of running a job to running a business. I became focused on what makes the cash register ring. It's much cheaper to hire people to do all the 'administrivia.'"

As for millionaire real-estate-broker-turned-mentor Valerie Fitzgerald of the Valerie Fitzgerald Group, she says what it takes to be a successful entrepreneur is to have a dream, a vision of what you want to do and why you want to do it. "My vision was so strong of creating a great life for my daughter, which meant a home and school and all those things that life could offer. I remember making a list of what those things would be for me and for her, and that was my vision. I create these "vision boards"; that was my vision board of what I was going to do to provide for my daughter instead of taking a different path. I could have gotten married along the way, I could have married someone much older who could take care of me financially, but that didn't suit me. I wasn't looking to be saved. I think what you need is a dream, to have a plan, to have goals.

Motivation

"If you change your thinking you can change your life."

Joyce Bone

Use the areas below to write your thoughts.

CHAPTER THREE

Overcoming Fear

*Fear grows in darkness; if you think there's a
bogeyman around, turn on the light.*

Dorothy Thompson,
the "First Lady of American Journalism"

As a child, I was fearful that an alligator lived under my bed at night and that if I got out of bed it might get me. Over time, I learned some fears, unlike others I would encounter later in life, had no basis in reality. Then as a teenager I spent five years on a diving team facing a much more common—and rational—fear. Because I was a powerful athlete, but not the most graceful, the coach assigned me to the high-dive board. Many people are afraid of even *being* at that height, let alone jumping from it. And in order to make state competition I had to do 2.5 pike front flips from the equivalent of a one-story building. Was I fearful? You'd better believe it! But I soon learned how to turn that fear into exhilaration, which had the added bonus of enhancing my diving performances. Fortunately, I also survived. It was during this time that I became proficient at quieting most fears in my head. It's not that you don't have them. It's just that you don't allow the thought to linger and grow. Once you get out of the habit of worrying, it's hard to get back into it since it's such a drag. After all, the vast majority of fears never come to pass!

Fear of Failure

As a 28-year-old transitioning from stay-at-home mom to corporate CEO in a rapidly expanding business, I encountered lots of opportunities for fear. Part of the plan involved securing funding for our company's fast-paced growth, and we decided to use a private-placement memorandum to raise $13 million dollars. Fifty accredited investors—all men—had flown in from around the country to listen to our pitch and were sitting around the boardroom table when my partner suddenly announced that I would be covering the financial projections. It was the one part of the plan I was the least prepared to present! As I waited for my turn, fear began to invade my thoughts and I started having trouble breathing. Here I was, young and female, about to stand in front of a group of savvy businessmen and essentially "wing" a discussion of financial projections—a discussion that could make or break a $13-million boost in funding! Finally, it occurred to me how ridiculous it would look for the only woman in the room to faint, and refusing to feed *that* stereotype I pulled myself together and did what had to be done. The funny thing is, after the meeting, several people told me what a great job of presenting I had done. What was more important from my perspective was that we raised the funds we needed. And I took away an important lesson from my fear that day: always be well prepared for any presentation; winging it is for rookies. Never again did I want to be uncomfortable speaking in front of a crowd, so I took action and completed a Toastmasters course. As a result, I've come to *enjoy* public speaking.

One of the women interviewed during the course of writing *Millionaire Moms* was Karen Waisath. She started Gold Canyon Candles as a way to stay home with her children. She and her husband used a home equity line and credit cards to fund their business. If they had failed, they would have lost their house and would have amassed huge amounts of debt. This was a young family. The ramifications of failing would have been huge.

Karen admitted she was terrified but gazed at her daughter's picture every day to focus and ground herself. It was a reaffirming way to remember there was no option but to make it work. Today, Gold Canyon is an enormously successful, multi-million dollar business employing hundreds of people.

Karen's advice to others on a similar path is to "Jump in feet first. Otherwise you won't have the commitment required to make it happen." I think this advice sums up entrepreneurial fear nicely. You will be scared. It can be isolating. You will experience unexpected, unpredictable bumps in the road. Obstacles will appear at every turn. The bottom line is that you have to stay one hundred percent committed to what you are doing.

"Our doubts are traitors and make us lose the good we often might win, by fearing to attempt."

Jane Addams, first American woman to receive the Nobel Peace Prize

---

What happens when a big decision must be made that can either grow or cripple a business? This is when the fear of the unknown and of making the wrong choice can be palpable. Debbie Shwetz and Dena Tripp from Nothing Bundt Cakes agonized over a decision to rebrand their business prior to franchising. Debbie explained, "The decision to franchise our company, Nothing Bundt Cakes, was the beginning of an incredible adventure through completely uncharted territory. However, nothing compared to the decision to re-brand our company. Our original brand seemed to be working. We were six months into the franchising process and on the brink of selling our first location when we began working with a company called Lunabrand Design Group on photography for our franchise brochures. Lunabrand talked with us for several hours about exactly what a brand was and suggested attending a brand workshop to really investigate our consumer messaging. The cost to attend the workshop was $2000, a substantial investment in an unknown. We were fearful over the cost and time involved, as money was very tight and we were well on our way to selling our first franchise. In the end we went to achieve a better understanding of the branding process.

"After attending the workshop we realized we had several disconnects in our existing brand. Our brand could be easily copied and offered too many opportunities for franchisee interpretation. We also realized the opportunity existed to elevate our product into a luxury brand. This could be accomplished prior to actually selling a franchise. The problem was it would cost us about $100,000 to completely rebrand and would delay our franchise sales by nine months to one year. In essence, we were starting over. We were so close to selling a franchise already. What a huge decision this was for us!

"The biggest problem was we had no guarantee we would even like the new brand. We were buying a concept rather than something concrete. It was going to cost a lot of money and delay our entire franchising progress. We talked, argued, cried, disagreed and agonized. After much deliberation we decided it was the best decision to go through the re-branding process before we sold a franchise.

"We are so thankful that we moved in this direction! Our stores are beautiful, our concept is systemized and simple, and the designs are proprietary. We have a guideline for operation that will last us for years and years. We were terrified of making that decision! To spend $100,000 on something that could not be truly measured was the biggest leap of faith we have ever taken. Now we can't imagine working under our old brand. The fear of the unknown almost crippled us, but the reality is we would have been crippled if we had not made this decision.

We learned that in business not everything can be measured, especially when making decisions in the areas of advertising and marketing. We also learned to overcome our fear, trust our instincts and take into account what our trusted advisors say. This combination can elevate your business to new levels of success. It is so comforting to know we can be fearful and move forward in spite of it. We don't have to have all the answers."

Fear of Rejection

Have you ever had to make a sales call over the phone? Did you pick up the phone to dial, then set it back down a few times before you mustered up the guts to call? Or perhaps you shuffle all the papers on your desk a few hundred times or empty the office trashcan prior to getting down to business? There are innumerable avoidance techniques to keep us from facing what we are uncomfortable doing. The real shame is that the vast majority of what we worry about never even happens. What a waste of energy!

Quite often, what you'll find when you peel back the layers is that most fears have their roots in a concern of potential rejection. No one enjoys being rejected. But look what happens when we reframe our thinking about the things that frighten us.

Stop a moment and consider whether there is something you want but are too fearful to ask for. It doesn't have to be big, just anything you're reluctant to request for yourself. As it stands, you are already rejected. By virtue of not having the courage to ask for what you want, you've voluntarily accepted an answer of "no". But if you assert yourself and put your request to the person who can help make it happen, one of two things will transpire: (1) you can get a "no", in which case your current situation hasn't changed, except now you *know* that person is not going to help you; or (2) you get what you seek. Congratulations! Doesn't that feel fantastic?! Not only have you obtained the desired result, but your self esteem has gotten a nice little boost.

Another way to reframe fearful thinking is to look at it statistically, which is how most business results are measured. If you are trying to sell something, for example, you may have to talk to 10 people before finding one who will say "yes". And let's say that "yes" puts $1,000 in your pocket. Then how about picturing the first nine "no" answers as putting $100 each in your pocket—sort of like deposits toward the full amount? Do you see the difference in perspective?

By taking no action, we surrender our lives to other people's agendas and choices. Make a habit of asking yourself not only what's the worst that could happen, but also what's the *best* possible outcome? What would you do, for example, if you knew it was impossible for you to fail? The answer might surprise you. And rather than dismiss it, dig a little deeper to find out what fears are keeping you from pursuing it. Here's the story of one of my millionaire moms who kept asking herself what the best possible outcome would be to her actions.

Barbara Carey is an inventor with more than 100 products in her current repertoire. When she first started trying to sell her wares to major retail stores, she refused to let fear of rejection take over. In her own words, Barbara recounts what happened: "I always had a calling to make things. I made a Halloween disguise. I called it an invention, but it was more of an idea. Fortunately for me, nobody told me that you needed an appointment with retailers. I decided to drive to Troy, Michigan from St. Louis, Missouri without any scheduled appointments. I couldn't afford a hotel so I slept in my car and lived on a jar of peanut butter and a loaf of bread. Once I arrived in Troy, I called the buyer from a major store and talked my way past the buyer's assistant to the buyer himself. It was 17 days before Halloween. He called me a "piece of work" when I told him my idea and that I had driven all this way to share it with him. He gave me a courtesy appointment. In return, I gave him the very best 'dog-and-pony show' I knew how to do. He said 'no'. I asked him, 'Why?' He said because it was too close to Halloween, but he loved the item. I persisted, 'If your boss said yes, would you say yes?' And he said he would. We went to go see his boss, and his boss said 'No'. I asked him the same question: If your boss said yes would you say yes? All three of us went to see the merchandise manager, and he said 'Yes'. In seven days I shipped my very first product, and it was to K-Mart. They gave me a receipt with good terms. I was paid in ten days. Within three weeks it was a million-dollar product line and I was able to fly home."

What might happen, then, if, like Barbara Carey, we redefine fear as "Focus-Effectiveness-Action-Release," so that our fears actually spur us to action instead of stymieing us from moving forward towards success?

The Many Faces of Fear

Don't be afraid to go out on a limb. That's where the fruit is.

H. Jackson Browne, Jr., American author

In talking with the millionaire moms I interviewed for this book, I was not surprised that none would describe herself as fearless. What was both enlightening and uplifting was to learn how they dealt with and often even harnessed their fears to their advantage. Two themes that emerged were faith and giving back to the community by helping others.

Elon Bomani confesses that she had a self-fulfilling prophesy of her greatest fear, which was that she would find herself divorced and have to raise her son by herself. "People know about 'The Secret,'" she said. "You repeat what you don't want to happen, and guess what? It manifests in your life." By focusing on her worst fear, she actually attracted it. But rather than choosing to see herself as a powerless victim, Elon decided to change her philosophy about how she perceived herself and take control of her financial, personal and spiritual destiny. Without a job or place to live, she reasoned she was already down so low she couldn't do anything but go up. "So even though I was homeless," she recalls, "I was not helpless." About her own rags-to-riches story of going from homeless, with just $36.00 in her checking account, to a net worth of more than $1 million in a year and a half, she says, "I realized that if God's going to provide for the birds, bees, flowers and trees, sure enough God will provide for me. But I had to step out on faith."

Cordia Harrington, founder, CEO and President of Tennessee Bun Company, relies on her faith and strong gut instincts to know what to do and evaluate what sacrifices are needed to succeed. "So when fear sets in," she advises, "it's really important to remember the purpose, which is for all of us to help each other to be our best, to know that sacrifices are going to need to be made and be willing to see the best and see the hope and go for it."

For Shelley Sun, knowledge is what provides the power to overcome. "I am a big believer in reading what you don't know about," she says, noting that the two books she found most helpful as she and her husband went about building BrightStar Healthcare were *Franchising for Dummies* and *Street Smart Franchising*. She also joined and started attending meetings of the International Franchise Association. When asked if she would have done anything differently, Shelley replied, "I wish I had started reading and attending meetings a year before we started franchising."

In Nadja Piatka's experience, it's not always fear of rejection or failure that stops us in our tracks; sometimes it's fear of success. Like Elon Bomani, she knows how self-fulfilling thoughts can be when we listen to the negative chatter in our heads. It's easy to fall into the trap of thinking you don't know enough, or have enough money to get started, or that your dreams are too big and unrealistic ever to come true. "Don't limit," Nadja advises. "I know one thing: if you set limitations, then you will meet them. Do not set any limitations." Starting out as an unemployable, single mother with two children to support and a bankroll of only $100, Nadja "hired" herself to create healthy recipes that also tasted good and has grown her kitchen-based start-up into an international supplier to Subway, McDonald's Canada, and food-service vendors and grocery stores across Canada and the U.S. "Don't be afraid of successes," she counsels, "or of the financial benefits, because you can do amazing things with them." One way to overcome that fear—especially for women, who can sometimes feel more comfortable thinking about others than themselves—is to concentrate on the bigger picture of what your success could mean.

"What I think is the most wonderful part of being successful is your ability to give back, to make society, your community and the world better. The bag lady in the park pushing her cart may have the biggest heart and soul in the whole world, but she won't be able to make a difference like someone who is in a financial position to really help people."

It is worth noting some people have a fear of success. When you become successful people in your inner circle and community can actually be hurtful at times. All of a sudden you are on the outside of their comfort zone. It can even cause marital difficulties. Sometimes the dynamic between partners shifts as do expectations. These can cause discord. Communication is key in this situation.

One thing the millionaire moms have in common is generosity. Examples include Sandra Yancey's foundation that provides grants and awards in support of women and children. Nadja Piatka wrote a cookbook and donated all the proceeds to the Ronald McDonald House and has provided funds to war widows throughout the world. Lucie Voves of Church Hill Classics, a diploma and certificate frame company, creates scholarships for students. Each woman has her own personal vision of how to make the world a better place, and they all have the funds to help. Another reason to become a millionaire mom!

Fear of Change

Change may be scary but it doesn't have to be a bad thing. In fact, more times than not it ultimately leads to better things. How many people have you heard say "I got fired, and it was the best thing that ever happened to me!"? Or those who have gone through the pain of divorce only to feel fantastic about the decision once they readjusted? The problem is we usually can't see that far ahead, and the unknown is scary!

Some of us were forced into entrepreneurship when we faced a drastic change in our lives. Initially, it can be intimidating trying to determine whether this new course is truly the best fit for you and your family. Many of us might never have had enough drive or confidence to make the change voluntarily without life circumstances giving us a helping hand. While Christy Clarke, founder of Table Topics, voluntarily chose this new path, she shared that it felt like she was leaving a life in which she felt competent in her everyday work to pursue a business where she knew almost nothing. "At 39 years old, I was extremely uncomfortable with becoming a beginner all over again, and this discomfort made me fearful of my ability to stick with it. I was also overwhelmed by the sheer number of things I needed to accomplish and at which I had to become proficient. I solved both problems by creating a long list of absolutely everything I needed to do in order to launch Table Topics. I prioritized the list and did a few things every day. This kept me from getting too overwhelmed on a day-to-day basis. I focused only on what I needed to accomplish that day. I also tried to remember that my growth would be a direct result of having put myself into some uncomfortable situations. And after staying at home with my kids for 10 years, I was ready to grow!"

A business is a living and changing entity. Nature grows and dies, and so do businesses. As the architects of our own lives, entrepreneurs tend to take these changes personally, but they are, in fact, just business. Evolution makes us stronger, faster and wiser. As comfortable as it is to feel like you know exactly what is going to happen next, it will never be a permanent state in any area of our lives. Those who not only survive but *thrive* are masters at adapting. This is reality. The sooner you come to terms with this, the better your chances of success.

In today's marketplace, you should be clear about what your business is and what it isn't; why people do business with you and why they don't; what works and what doesn't; who works and who doesn't. It's important to accept what you can and cannot control when facing a change. Some factors are out of our hands no matter how hard we try to control our environment. The skills and abilities you've honed in the past, however, will remain assets to you in this ever-changing world. Just be willing to use them in new and inventive ways! If your reason, your "why" is strong enough, it will serve as an anchor during turbulent times. Open yourself up to the new possibilities and opportunities. They are a gift. You may need to rethink the best way to achieve your purpose, but hold true to your underlying dream.

While it can feel hopeless and downright horrible to experience change, in the end it often proves to be the magical turning point in our lives. Many feel truly grateful once we get clear of the storms. My mother always told me *every cloud has a silver lining*. It may be a cliché, but it is true! Let times of change act as evolution towards better outcomes. Our destiny is in our responses to life's events.

One of my motivations for writing this book and creating MillionaireMoms.com was to shed light on the fact that you are good enough *today* to start creating the life you secretly dream of. It doesn't matter who laughs in your face, what you think you "should" do, who supports you or who doesn't. What does matter is what *you think*. Success is not reserved for the fearless, it is for the courageous. Fear is a part of being human. The courageous among us step into the arena in spite of the fear. It is when we are most fearful that we experience the most growth. Most of life is ho hum. Here's an idea: Why don't we reframe fear into a sense of exhilaration? It is when we are most uncomfortable that we are experiencing the most growth. When victorious we can celebrate our ability to overcome!

Shoot for the moon. Even if you miss, you'll land among the stars.

Brian Littrell, American singer/songwriter

How Do I Overcome Fear?

WORD PICTURE JUMBLE

This puzzle is a cryptogram. You will need to use the key to reveal the hidden phrase. Here is a little clue regarding the phrase. **Hint** – apples

Instructions: Use the key below to unscramble the letters to reveal the phrase in the word picture jumble. For instance, use A for the ♨ and B for ●. In other words, each letter is represented by a little picture. You will use the Word Picture Key to unscramble the Word Picture Jumble Puzzle. The phrase is something you read in chapter two. It is our hope that by trying your hand at this puzzle, you will more easily remember this important phrase.

Word Picture Key

A	B	C	D	E	F	G	H	I	J
♨	●	♫	👁	✕	🚌	Ⓨ	👄	⛑	♫
K	**L**	**M**	**N**	**O**	**P**	**Q**	**R**	**S**	**T**
🕷	👂	🏍	👤	🖂	🎧	✋	💰	🐞	🔓
U	**V**	**W**	**X**	**Y**	**Z**				
🎿	🚎	📚	★	🗿	🗄				

Word Picture Jumble Puzzle

Okay. Ready? Here's the puzzle. We included some of the letters to give you a jump start.

🔓	👄	♨	🔓		⛑	🐞		
	H							
📚	👄	✕	💰	✕				✕
W	H					T	H	
🚌	💰	🎿	⛑	🔓		⛑	🐞	
F		U		T				

- 52 -

CHAPTER FOUR

Time Management

*Perhaps the very best question that you can
memorize and repeat, over and over, is, 'What is
the most valuable use of my time right now?'*

Brian Tracy, Trainer &
Personal Development Expert

The Fabulousness of "Fit"

Do you know anyone who doesn't need more time in their day?
Women entrepreneurs are especially time-starved. We juggle so many
competing responsibilities that it's hard to stay focused on anything!
What do we do when we have so much to do? The answer to this
conundrum involves "fit."

Fit is a great word with which to replace "balance." It just works.
When you are *fit* you are healthy. We *fit* things into our schedule that
matter to us. It is a powerful word that leaves you in control. Why not
start applying fit to all areas of your life? The importance of being fit in
business, family and self is a concept to which we all can relate. Find
work that fits your personality and passion. Be sure to fit your family
needs in before everything else, as it is these relationships that matter
the most. It's important to remember to take a deep breath and think
about the right choices for *your* situation. Life is a marathon, not a

sprint. You *can* have it all—just not all at once. If you approach life with this sensibility, you will find more peace.

Julie Lenzer Kirk, author of *The Parentpreneur Edge: What Parenting Teaches About Building a Successful Business,* reminds us, "All of life is about juggling, and it's your job to recognize which balls in the air are rubber and which ones are glass. The trick of it is, one day the kids can be absolutely glass if they are having an issue or there is something going on with them that I need to be there for. But at a different time it can be work that really needs my focus. Establish some criteria to help you figure it out."

Forget running yourself ragged trying to make it all work at once. Lovingly accept your choices. What's most important at this stage of life? Other areas will recede for the time being but not forever. It's about choices. The process of defining what is chosen puts a person in a position of power rather than that of victim of circumstances.

By staying in the moment and truly appreciating it, you will find that life becomes much sweeter. Balance, juggling, fit or whatever you want to call it tends to take care of itself once you subscribe to acting and thinking this way. It can take a while and perhaps feel awkward at first, but soon your life will be more peaceful and joyful in spite of a hectic schedule. Be sure to assess what is most valued at this stage of life; the ability to prioritize activities will naturally fall into place.

Ninety percent of the millionaire moms I have interviewed created their businesses and fortunes *after* having children? Why? The children were the motivation to create a flexible, profitable business in the first place! What is wonderful about being entrepreneurial is the ability to pay the bills and be available for our children. It doesn't have to be an "all-or-nothing" experience. Helping women figure out how to be financially independent and available to their children is the reason millionairemoms.com was created. Children can learn a great number of positive life skills from entrepreneurial parents.

There will be times when work consumes more of your day and attention than may be comfortable. The key is to build up your resources.

Learn to become a master communicator and negotiator. Who can lend a hand? Are you married? It's exponentially beneficial to get your spouse on board. He may have to help out more around the house, but I guarantee you he will like the checks rolling in! Communicate with everyone in a position to help you. Explain why it is in everyone's best interest to pitch in during these high-pressure times.

Flexibility is Key

As Natalie Kennedy from Kennedy Creative discovered, "Once I learned that even the best-laid plans can unravel at any moment, I became a much happier and calmer person! All it takes is one phone call from a client, one message that didn't get relayed, one sniffle from your kiddo and your entire schedule is changed. Playing on your strengths, leaning on your team and being realistic about your time are all key. Balancing comes from understanding that you can do it all—you just can't do it all at once."

Tory Johnson, founder of Women For Hire and Career Correspondent for ABC's "Good Morning America," echoes the notion of flexibility as crucial. She says, "No two days are alike. Many days I walk in with one agenda in my mind and I get a call from "Good Morning America" wanting a segment for the next day. This requires me to shuffle my whole day around. Other times, someone is out sick, so I end up doing a lot of their job for the day. It's always an adventure."

It seems peace of mind and flexibility are integral parts of time management for working moms. It affords us the opportunity to accomplish our goals in a centered way. We will have obstacles thrown at us. It is our job to recognize, as parents and as businesswomen, that each day can turn out differently than planned. The variables beyond our control will be challenging, but we can choose our response. Therein lies the power!

Millionaire mom Erika Andersen is the owner of Proteus International, founded in 1980. They offer business advice and have become known for promoting learning and change in ways uniquely tailored to her clients' challenges, goals and culture. Erika says, "I tend to be good at managing my time, and I'm convinced it's because I consistently make the effort to 'pull back the camera' and look at my current situation as a whole. Then it's pretty easy to figure out what's most important to do, how to 'pattern' my effort to reduce redundancy and take advantage of potential synergies, and how to let/encourage/request other people to do things I don't need to do myself!"

Early Risers

How many times have we heard the cliché "the early bird gets the worm"? Here's a question to ponder: "What about the worm?" All kidding aside, it's true that those who get up early really get things done. There is something magical about those early hours, especially for moms. *No one* bothers you at 5 a.m., not even the dog. Many of the millionaire moms I interviewed attest to this as well.

Kristi Frank, Season One contestant on TV's "The Apprentice" and founder of Girl's Guide to Online Success, says, "I have seen a huge increase in productivity and cash flow by capitalizing on the times when I am most creative and powerful. For me that's in the very beginning of the day. I don't turn on my email accounts. I save that for the end of the day when my son has gone to sleep. It's become a more relaxed, mindless surfing activity. I do my most productive activities first thing in the morning, and that's definitely not email." Shelly Sun from BrightStar Healthcare is a super successful millionaire mom. She says, "My biggest challenge is finding the time to answer the 200 emails that come in each day and return the 25 phone calls, plus get everything else done. I am trying to put people in place to change that. I need to focus on being the CEO more hours of the day."

You will be more profitable if you focus on growing your business rather than getting caught up in the administrative functions.

Have a Daily Agenda

There are many different ways to organize your day-to-day activities. Here are examples of how two of our millionaire moms do it:

Nancy Jane "NJ" Goldston is the founder and Chief Executive Officer of THE UXB™, an award-winning, world-class advertising, branding and interactive agency. Goldston directs creative and branding strategies for a variety of emerging brands and Fortune 500 companies.

Here is what NJ does to keep it all going: "When it comes to managing kids, family and The UXB, making lists has always been my biggest organizational tool. I divide my lists into four different groups each day and work my way through each list of ten items categorized as action items, follow-up items, personal tasks and phone calls, with the phone numbers listed. I distinctly separate the work tasks from the personal tasks and block time that way. This way I always feel at the end of the day I achieved real results at work and have more time for family."

Diane Kuehn, President and CEO of VisionPoint Marketing, an Internet marketing agency for mid-size organizations that provides strategy, creative services and execution of integrated online marketing programs, describes her preferred method of planning: "Some people may think of me as Type A, but on Sunday evening I outline my entire week in an Excel spreadsheet. Every item is categorized as the type of activity (sales, management, marketing, etc.), the date that it needs to be done, and the item. Then I print out the spreadsheet and keep the hard copy with me the entire week as I check off what's been done, what is in process, and add new items to the list. At the end of each week, I copy the previous week's electronic copy to a new spreadsheet and make my updated plan for the next week. There have been a few weeks in the year where I was unable to "organize my weekly list," and I know my productivity level dropped dramatically. The list allows me to spend 15 minutes on planning my week only once. The rest of the week is focused on executing the plan."

Find an approach that resonates with you. The point is, plan the work. Ten minutes of planned time will save you 20 minutes winging it. If you are serious about running a business and a family at the same time, it is a fundamental step. It's as simple as that.

Laser Focus

The magic happens after the "to do" list has been created. This is where the girls are separated from the women, Ladies. It is so easy to get caught up in the "busyness" of life. The question is can you break through this cycle and be effective? There is a huge difference between doing a lot and being effective. Millionaire moms and millionaire moms-in-training want to be effective! Act with purpose and a plan and you will attract opportunities.

Have you ever heard of the Pareto Principle? It's also known as the 80/20 rule. There are many ways to apply this principle to life, but for our purposes, let's think of it this way: 80 percent of your results come from 20 percent of your actions. It's up to you to figure out the 20 percent of your "to do'" list that will give you the greatest gains in business and with your family. Focus on those activities first. Before you know it, you will be making fantastic strides towards success!

Sandra Yancey, founder of eWomen Network, brings up an excellent point regarding focus. It's important to stay dialed in on what our area of genius is and do that as much as possible. Sandra also points out that it's better to give up some of the business in order to grow it. One hundred percent of a business generating zero is still zero. It makes more sense to be willing to share in order to grow.

Here is what Sandra had to say: "I wanted to focus on doing the things that I do best, which was spreading the word, showing the vision, and gaining membership. I told my assistant I wanted to make her a partner. I gave her four percent of the business. What I learned in the process is that I would rather have 96 percent of millions and millions and millions of dollars than 100 percent of nothing."

Sharmen Lane is an author, speaker, radio host and life coach. She has trained, managed and coached thousands of individuals on what it takes to get what they want. *The 7 Secrets to Create Your Fate*, which is a personal growth and self development book, is what launched Sharmen from manicurist to millionaire. Sharmen has five steps for time management:

1. Write
    Everything you need or want to get done in a day, write it down. This will free up your mind and allow you to be more focused and accomplish more.

2. Eliminate distractions
    Distractions or interruptions are the primary cause for many of our inefficiencies. Get what needs to be done, done.

3. Stay in the moment
    Many times people do not use the present moment effectively because they are projecting in the future or dwelling on the past. Here's the thing–no matter how much you ponder and percolate on something that has already happened, it isn't going to change it. Think about where you are now and what you can do in this present moment to make the best of any situation.

4. Set an alarm
    If you need to get something done in a specific amount of time or if you need to dedicate minutes or hours to a project in order to complete it by the deadline, set an alarm. Allotting a specific amount of time will enable you to concentrate on just the matter at hand without concerning yourself with the clock or other things around you.

5. Reward yourself
    Nothing is better than having a little incentive when you are learning a new habit. Now you'll have an enticement to stay focused, avoid distractions and get what needs to be done, done.

Passion For Profit

Margery Kraus is President and Chief Executive Officer of APCO Worldwide, which she founded in 1984. She has transformed it from a company with one small Washington office to a multinational consulting firm in major cities throughout the Americas, Europe, the Middle East, Africa and Asia. APCO is one of the largest privately owned communication and public affairs firms in the world.

"If you really enjoy your work, it's easier to dedicate the necessary time to make it a success. When I started this business, I knew it was something I really wanted to do, something I enjoy, and something I'm good at. Doing my job means I'm doing what I love. Because of that, I don't become exhausted, even when the days are long.

On a more practical level, I really do love my Blackberry. I try to stay as organized as possible so that I don't waste time looking for what I need or duplicating work I've already done. Also, having employees whom you really trust and can depend on is the best time management tip of all. There is no way I could manage everything alone." Margery brings up a good point. We can't do it all on our own. We need to protect our best and biggest investment: ourselves.

Keep the Engine Running

Time management means taking control of the various aspects of life. If we don't recharge ourselves we won't be effective and we won't be happy.

Resist the urge to run yourself into the ground. If your business is new and you can't afford employees yet, it's time to consider alternatives. Can an intern from a local university help you? Call and find out. At most schools you can find free help or pay a nominal fee. This is only one suggestion. Put your creative mind to work! There are many moms who would love flexible, part time work to earn a little extra. It never hurts to investigate your options.

Take the Time to Take Care of #1

We need to take care of ourselves in order to be available for our families. This is simple but worth stating, as our nature is to overextend ourselves.

Find the time to exercise and eat right. These two components are the foundation for life. The results of neglecting our bodies are evident for the world to see: flabby arms and legs, dark circles under the eyes from lack of sleep, dull skin from too little water. Vibrancy is intoxicating. You will be rewarded many times over for giving yourself this gift.

If it's a struggle to incorporate healthy changes into your routine, start off easy. Even simple steps create positive differences over time. For example, commit to eliminating fast food from your diet or always take the stairs instead of the elevator. A car stops when it runs out of gas. The human body is similar—we have to replenish it regularly whether we want to or not!

Nadja Piatka had cancer and understands how essential it is to commit the time to maintaining her own health and fitness. She states, "We get overly scheduled and tend to multitask all those demands of life. I have found I must dedicate an hour to myself each day to work out. I come back refreshed. It is really instrumental for me. The times I ignored this need are the times when everything seemed to suffer. I find it actually helps me with my time management in the long run."

Kayla Fioravanti is Vice President, Chief Formulator, ARC-Registered & Certified Aromatherapist for Essential Wholesale and its lab division, Essential Labs. Here's Kayla's perspective on well-being: "Absolutely the most important thing I have found to maximize my time is to eat a healthy diet, exercise and drink plenty of water. It makes me more energized, gives me better focus and helps me sleep at night. When we started out, I put those things aside. I felt awful and was dragging all the time. When I added exercise and a healthy organic diet to my day, I found that I got so much more done. I am busier than I have ever been, but making the time to take care of myself has been the secret to optimizing my time."

Family

Time management for parents is a completely different paradigm from that of our pre-kid days. Gone is any sense of singular. We live in a plural world! We now have to accommodate our children's needs, desires and schedules in addition to our own. The more children you have, the dicer this gets. We are limited to 24 hours in a day! Many times, I've heard other women say, "If I didn't have kids, I could _____." This is a fallacy. Remember, the vast majority of millionaire moms made their fortunes *after* having children. The kids were the motivators.

Ariana Reed runs her own successful business and simultaneously home-schools six children. If she can do it, anyone can! Ariana attributes schedules as the formula for success in time management. Her words of advice: "Prioritize. My days are hectic until about 9 or 10 a.m. I trained my children from the time they were two, to do the same repetitive actions every morning. We have an established routine and chore charts complete with Polaroid pictures. They are to get up, get dressed, put their dirty clothes in the laundry basket, brush their hair, brush their teeth, wash their faces, go back to their rooms and make their beds, bring their laundry baskets downstairs all the way to the basement. They use the color codes on their laundry baskets in order to sort their own laundry. And they each do one morning chore. Meanwhile, I make breakfast for everyone. It takes some training, but if you start instilling this type of routine when kids are two, they are totally independent with no assistance by the age of four."

Ariana continues, "What are our goals today? What are some concerns we might have for the day? Here is how I would like to present them. We focus on the family every morning during breakfast. Then we start school. The first thing is always reading. Everybody has to do one hour of reading which allows me to check my voice mail, download my email, pour myself a cup of coffee. It's quite interesting that, for our family, home schooling is easier than going to school. I teach for 15 to 20 minutes, and then they do independent work for 15 to 20 minutes. I work my business until the early afternoon in 15 to 20 minute segments. Isn't that's interesting?"

For many, constantly switching between different tasks could prove difficult. If you find yourself in this position, it's helpful to group similar tasks in order to minimize the transition time it typically takes to get into a productive state of mind. Ariana says, "Every day I make it a goal to spend one hour searching for people with common interests and goals. I then send them an invitation through a social networking site to become my friend or my connection." This helps her grow her people-centered business.

So here's the million-dollar question: If this home schooling mom of six can become a millionaire mom, what's holding you back? What's noteworthy is how a mom of six would take an hour out of her day to connect with people. The saying "it's not what you know, it's who you know" comes to mind. Let's face it, all things being equal, it's true. *People*, more than ideas, make business happen.

Messages from the "Tweeples"

How do you meet new people daily? Social networking is the answer. It is gaining popularity at exponential rates. The face of the Internet and how marketing works have been dramatically changed. Besides, it's just plain fun! Home-based entrepreneurs and employees now have an efficient way to connect with the outside world. I am a fan of Twitter. Their site has grown 900 percent this year alone, with no signs of slowing. I love the immediate feedback it offers. For instance, I asked for time-management tips recently and within five minutes received these responses:

Parents4Change@MillionaireMoms prep as many meals together as possible, i.e., huge freezer day 1x month, prep dinner while getting kids breakfast or lunch.

specialedsolved@MillionaireMoms Sometimes taking a 10 minute break to play with the kids actually helps productivity and keeps everyone happy.

MzLimitless@MillionaireMoms Using Outlook helps greatly with time management in terms of scheduling appointments, making task lists, keeping journals, coordinating w/email integration.

specialedsolved@MillionaireMoms Most people are in bed for 8 hours and work for 8 hours. It's what YOU do with the other 8 hours that makes the difference.

JustWrite@MillionaireMoms - On Time Mgt/Sleep Deprivation-If UR going 2 B tired ANYWAY, go ahead & get up 30 minutes earlier 4 a few moments o' peace.

galel Never save a voicemail message. It's a waste of time. When listening to voicemails, write down what you need and DELETE.

NickDeStefano@MillionaireMoms keep small recorder by bed...1st thing in morning thoughts are generally DREAM solutions to problems.

MetroDance@MillionaireMoms Make a list of your top 3 things to do each day. Focus on those first thing in the morning. All the rest is bonus.

MaryRichmond@MillionaireMoms if I don't write it down and schedule it then it may become lost forever....;-) lists save me hours and hours.

tracilove@MillionaireMoms forget multi-tasking; it's inefficient. Work on one thing at a time & focus on it 100% (if possible; tough for moms!)

NatalieTM@MillionaireMoms Managing energy and not focusing on the time factor.

lacreshahayes@MillionaireMoms Tip: Do the most time consuming, stressful or important jobs first. We're more alert in the morning.

CathyBend@MillionaireMoms I keep a timer by my computer. I allow myself a certain amt of time for emails, twitter, forums, etc, between work projects.

ChattyMamaBear@MillionaireMoms I normally am scatter-brained, so I have to write a to-do list in my day timer, and set the timer for certain tasks.

JacquelineGates@MillionaireMoms Use a timer for EVERYTHING! Decide on a limit, focus on ONE thing, and change tasks when timer goes off. Works for kids too!

Twitter is part resource and part community. It is the modern day version of the office water cooler. If you decide to join or are a member already be sure to follow me @millionairemoms. It can be a tool if you use it as one. You can get quick answers. Just be sure to set limits. It's easy to get sucked into the "twitterverse" and waste time!

We are not robots and we need to step back and take a moment here and there during the day. You can use social networking sites with a "stick and carrot" mentality. Use them as a reward if you accomplish your goal. For instance, "If I finish writing this chapter I will reward myself with 10 minutes on Twitter." Not a bad plan!

Get Organized

Here are some "down and dirty" tips from organizational expert Lorie Marrero. She is a Certified Professional Organizer and the Creator of ClutterDiet.com. Her book, *"The Clutter Diet, The Skinny on Organizing Your Home and Taking Control of Your Life,"* is the definitive guide to running an efficient, organized household. Many working moms struggle trying to keep the house running smoothly. I highly recommend her system. It certainly has been a help to me!

Delegate

Focus on what you do best and delegate the rest. You may realize that your spouse, your children, and others around you are more capable than you thought. Make sure you (1) clearly communicate what needs to be done, (2) empower the person to get it done, and (3) follow up with that person to make sure it was done.

Configure appointments to avoid traffic

If you have a choice between getting a haircut at 8:30 or at 9:30, it may be wiser to choose 9:30 so you will avoid much of the morning logjam. Is there a way you could have a more flexible schedule at work? Is there a way you could work from home in the mornings and come in later after traffic slows down? Think about avoiding rush hour as much as possible to save tremendous amounts of time in your car and lots of money on gas. (Reduce your "carbon footprint" too!)

Consolidate errands

Make a list of errands in your time management system, all grouped together for better visibility. If you need to go out, look at your errands list to see what else can be done in the same outing. Clutter Diet members know about the recommendation to have a "Destination Station" with a shelf for errand items, so they stay near the door ready to go out with you.

Use a timer

One of the best time management tools is a simple kitchen timer. You can do anything for short spans of time – ten minutes, 15 minutes, or even one hour, depending on the task. Break procrastination by promising yourself you only have to do a finite amount and then you can take a break to check e-mail or do something else you think is fun. You may find that you want to continue beyond the bell. Another timer method is trying to "beat the clock" with something you want to get through quickly, like doing the dishes. You can also use a timer to limit lengthy phone conversations, another big time stealer!

Trade time with a friend

Teaming up with others can save you both a lot of time. Ask a nearby friend to be an "errand buddy." When one of you goes to the grocery store or discount store, call and ask if the other person needs anything. Friends can also help each other with organizing projects and other big undertakings, and it makes the whole thing much more fun!

Think like a lazy person

Ask yourself, "How can I do this faster, better, or not at all?" Purposefully looking for efficiencies can yield huge time savings. Asking yourself, "How can I avoid cooking dinner?" means you might get more creative with some leftovers. Asking yourself, "How can I get to this meeting faster?" means you might find an alternate driving route that saves you ten minutes. Train your brain to think this way and you will be surprised what you can do in less time!

Say NO more often

Other people's priorities should not automatically be yours. When you are clear on your priorities, it's easier to say no to things that don't matter.

Shop online whenever possible

If it takes you 15 minutes to drive to the mall, ten minutes to park and go in, 30 minutes to walk around and shop, and another 15 minutes to drive home, you've spent more than an hour of your time. You've also spent money on gas to drive there and back. Perhaps you could perform the same transaction in only 15 minutes or less on your computer. Yes, you do have to pay for shipping, but you won't have to pay for gas, and you've gained back almost an hour of your time.

Pay your bills online, and have bills automatically paid whenever possible

It takes a lot of time to handle paper bills, write paper checks, and mail them in an envelope with a stamp. Most banks now have online bill paying capability, and it takes a fraction of the time to handle your payments. You can set up automatic recurring payments for things like your car loan, mortgage, even the orthodontist.

Consolidate and simplify credit card accounts

If you have multiple credit cards, try to pare down to just two—one for every day use and one for emergencies. If you have credit cards other than those, you are adding tremendously to the time it takes you to pay bills and reconcile accounts. Department store cards can be tempting when they offer you a good deal for opening an account, but use them only once to get "the deal" and then put them away.

Consolidate passwords in one secure location

People waste a lot of time trying to remember user names, passwords, account numbers, and other personal information they have forgotten. It's not secure to use the same password for everything, and you really should change passwords periodically as well

Buy low-maintenance clothing

Clothes that require special care, dry cleaning, or even ironing take a lot of time to maintain, and they can cost many times their original value in cleaning expenses. Why not buy no-iron slacks and other washable clothes? Think about this as you make clothing purchases. Some low-care fabrics may cost more, but you'll actually save money and time in the long run.

Use a shopping list

Everyone has experienced returning from the grocery store and realizing you've forgotten one or two important things. Going back to the store for those missed items is time-consuming and frustrating! Use a simple shopping list to help you reduce these trips and gain efficiency.

Avoid going to the post office with Click & Ship from the US Postal Service

If you are shipping Priority Mail or Express Mail, you can use Click & Ship online to print the postage you need. (www. usps.com, click "Print a Shipping Label") Also make sure you request a free pickup—your mail carrier will come up to your porch or wherever you specify to pick up your package and send it on its way. Stock up on Priority Mail boxes (for free!) and you're all set for shipping from home. No more long post office lines (especially during the holidays)!

Go paperless—and don't print

You can get just about anything in electronic form now, whether it's a phone bill or your medical insurance benefits statements. Why not receive items electronically and save them to your hard drive without printing? Any time you create a paper document you are making more work for yourself to sort, file, review, shred and purge that paper later.

Get expert advice

If you need to get something done, instead of learning it from scratch yourself, get an expert to handle the situation. For example, if your taxes are complicated, you might spend some agonizing time reviewing IRS tax codes to figure out what to do, when a CPA would instantly know how to address your issues correctly. It's worth it to pay someone who does this every day to save you all of that time and energy.

Drastically cut your television watching time

Did you know that, according to Nielsen Media, the average American watches four and a half hours of TV per day? (source: www.tvturnoff.org) That's more than 30 hours per week! Imagine what you could get done if you cut down even by half…that is a lot of "found" time.

Get up earlier

You can automatically add another 30 minutes or even an hour to your day simply by getting up earlier. You still need the same amount of sleep, but are you staying up late unnecessarily? Are you just watching Jay Leno or the news? If you go to bed earlier you can then wake up earlier and enjoy more productive time in your day.

My Millionaire Moms Shortcuts

The objective of being organized is to squeeze the maximum amount of time out of your day. Moms, perhaps more than others, need to be as efficient as possible. Becoming an organized person will help you accomplish your objectives. I'm always looking for the most direct path from point A to point B. Let's look at a few ways to save time "Millionaire Mom" style:

Desk Drawer

Keeping one or two "to do's" on your desk at any given moment. The rest go into a drawer until the task at hand is completed. The sense of "overwhelm" will disappear!

Cloud-Based Computing

I like using computer applications you can access from anywhere. Here are my three favorites:

1. Google Calendar

I've found this tool helpful in staying coordinated with my husband. We started utilizing Google calendar, and now we both know what's going on with each other and the kids with a click of the mouse. You can access this information from anywhere. The bonus is that you can allow others to view it as well. Grandparents, assistants, carpool pals can all view your calendar. This saves time on having to explain when you are and aren't available.

2. Google Docs

I really like Google docs when you are collaborating with people on a project. Simply post the document on the site and allow access to those involved. It is so much easier to track changes this way. No need to send endless attachments around.

3. Google Reader

This is a great place to consolidate blogs and other sites you follow in one place. No more clicking around all over cyberspace to keep up with your favorite reads!

Millionaire Moms Tricks of the Trade

More often than not, the trick to getting things done is staying out of eyesight and earshot of life's many distractions. Here are some you may not have thought of:

SlyDial

SlyDial lets you call directly to someone's voicemail. Isn't it wonderful having an underground method of bypassing that one person whom you would prefer avoiding? Everyone has a "Chatty Cathy" in her life. Do you need to get your point across without a 30-minute conversation? Try SlyDial. It's tricky. You simply send the recipient a message as you would an SMS message. It works on all the carriers.

With this technology, there are short advertisements before your calls are connected. These can be annoying, but the ads aren't nearly as long-winded as some people are! You can officially deliver your message in a hurry.

There's also no sign-up required; you simply have to call 267-SLY-DIAL (759-3425) and have the number of the person you're calling on hand. In the future, the service plans to offer a software application that can take advantage of your phone's contact list to save you from having to remember people's numbers.

Jott

Have you ever been out running errands or taking your kids to ballet, baseball, piano, or boy scouts and had a thought pop into your brain that you didn't want to forget? Now there is salvation! Jott makes sure you stay on top of everything. With a simple phone call to 866-JOTT-123, you can capture notes, set reminders and calendar appointments, stay in touch with friends and family, and interact with your favorite web sites and services...all with your voice! They can even transcribe your voicemail. Simply call Jott and tell them where you want your message to go. They capture your voice, turn it into text, and send it to the destination you chose.

More "I Need to Try That!" Tricks

Mini hour glass (5 minutes)

Crate & Barrel carries these gems. If an unexpected, unplanned phone call comes in, flip over the hourglass. It is a visual reminder that when the sand runs out, it is time to wind up the call.

Visual Cues

A visual reminder for family members that you are working can be quite helpful. One suggestion is to tie a brightly colored bandana to the door knob. It represents "Do Not Disturb!" unless it's an emergency.

Shop on Wednesdays

Surveys show that grocery stores are less crowded on this day, and shelves are likely to be well stocked.

Plan your meals in advance

More than half of those who cook dinner at home decide what to prepare that afternoon. Try creating a weekly menu and shop all at once. The added bonus is if you make a weeks' worth, then you don't have to think through the "What's for dinner" ordeal every day!

Eliminate All Distractions for a Set Time

Distractions are everywhere! They take the form of email, cell phone, the list is endless. Challenge yourself to find ways of cutting out all distractions for a set time. This is one of the most effective ways of getting things done in less time. You can't hide forever, but you can be nearly four times as productive while you are! Here's one suggestion: if you are struggling with hiding, go to a restaurant with Wi-fi for blocks of time. You won't have as many temptations as you do at home. Refuse to check email while you focus on your work.

Standardize Common Responsibilities

If you find yourself performing the same set of tasks on a regular basis then it makes sense to establish an efficient, standardized way of accomplishing them. It's up to you to find an efficient pattern, standardize it and follow it.

Productively Use Waiting Time

Waiting time does not have to be wasted time. When you are waiting at the doctor's office, the post office, or on hold for the next available representative, what simple tasks could you complete while you wait?

It might seem obvious but...

Make sure you claim an area as your own for personal work space.

Create your filing system.

Set it up whatever way works for you. You will save time not having to hunt for important files. I have two distinct businesses and, therefore, have two different colored file folders to distinguish between them. You can do the same. Again, do whatever is effective for you.

Just Do It

Let's face it, getting ready to get ready doesn't get the job done. Taking action gets the job done. Sometimes we have to discipline ourselves to get busy *doing* rather than *organizing*. Ready, Fire, Aim needs to be your mantra. You can always adjust but if you don't start, you get nowhere. Rather than waste time and mental energy procrastinating, wouldn't it be better to flip the switch on your brain and just do it? Don't even allow yourself to think about it. This tactic works in a number of areas.

Here is one example. I recently started a new exercise program and set my alarm for 6 a.m. I placed my running shoes and clothes at the end of the bed. The iPod was fully charged and ready by the garage door. When the alarm went off, I immediately hopped out of bed (no snooze button allowed!)

put on my gear, went outside, and started running. I didn't give myself the option of having a cup of coffee and checking email first. I know myself too well. Free thought would have meant getting involved at my desk and not running.

Having trouble figuring out where your time went? Keep a time log for a few days. That should straighten you out! Track accomplishments for one day. It's a visual reminder that productive things are happening.

Focus on the outcome

Life can be overwhelming with the never-ending demands on our time. When we feel defeated, procrastination sets in. A great mechanism to overcome this tendency is to focus on how empowering it will feel to have the project behind you! Visualize all the good things that will happen as a result of following through on your commitments.

When you love what you do, every day you get to do what you love. With that combination, time manages itself and it's never a problem.

Judi Sheppard Missett,
CEO of Jazzercise

Time Management

There was a word that was used quite a bit in the time management chapter. We think it is extremely important to your success. This puzzle helps you think about the word. *Instructions: There is a common prefix and suffix in each of these words. What is it?*

Pro____

____ness

Bene____

CHAPTER FIVE

Business Advice

Having spoken with nearly 100 millionaire moms, I've heard all kinds of business advice. This chapter evolved from conversations I've had with some of these fabulously successful women.

Before we hear their thoughts, I want to remind you that YOU CAN DO IT! All you need is to commit 100 percent. The rest will reveal itself along the way. If self defeating thoughts enter your mind, replace them with the positive self talk! It really makes a difference.

Many millionaire moms start out with all kinds of strikes against them, myself included. Let's review where I started my entrepreneurial journey. I was a stay at home mom. I did not have the funds necessary to start a business of this magnitude. Did I let that stop me? No. It was a solid idea with huge upside. I persisted in spite of the odds. My problems were solved by finding an investor/partner. I researched the opportunity and feed him information for six months until he was comfortable that it was in fact a great idea. What if I told myself, "Forget it, it's not realistic." Or, "I'm tired of doing all this research without any guarantees of a pay off." Where would I be now? Before giving up, ask yourself "Where will I be if I DON'T start my own business?" That can be a bigger fear than not trying!

Remember, most millionaire moms weren't the smartest in their class, nor did we have the resources with which to start. What we did do is "start." We took action. What all of us have in common is our drive. What impels us varies from woman to woman, but the common denominator is the desire for flexibility (both in time and resources) to raise our children the way we want.

Entrepreneurs can see what doesn't yet exist. Roy Disney was asked at the opening of Disney World if it saddened him to know Walt Disney couldn't see his dream become a reality. Roy responded, "We are here today precisely because Walt *could* see his dream as reality." Engage all your senses when thinking about your life and what you desire to create. It is effective and fun!

Be persistent and tenacious. Commitment to cause is what separates the wannabes from the accomplished. Do the important action daily. Each top priority step gets you closer to your goal. Communication is key to the success of any business, whether it's communication with employees, customers, other companies, the media or investors. *How* a business owner communicates is as important as *what* she communicates, and it's paramount to understand the nuances of every method and message. Study communication. It pays off in real dollars and better relationships over time.

Communication

Before we dive into business communication, let's remember it all starts with you as an individual.

You Are The Message

Good communication begins with good conversation. Whether you are leveraging your business or selling your product, you are the message. The book *You Are the Message – Getting What You Want by Being Who You Are* was written by Roger Ailes. You may never have heard of him, but you should incorporate his wisdom into your business practices. He's a media master who enjoyed an amazing television career and acted as Ronald Reagan's speech coach. His advice is timeless.

Roger emphasizes that polls have consistently shown that the ability to communicate well is ranked the number-one key to success by business leaders. That's huge! Commit yourself to becoming an excellent communicator. You have two ears and one mouth. Use them in that order.

Ask yourself, or better yet, have a friend or spouse answer these questions for you:

Are you self centered or other-oriented?

Do you talk too much?

Do you complain a lot?

Can you discuss subjects besides your kids or career track?

Is your speaking lively or monotone?

Do you ask open ended questions to draw people out?

Do you preach your opinion, or do you ask others how they feel?

Your goal is to be as engaging, empowering, and encouraging as you can in all your communications.

Things can move quickly from good to bad if there is faulty or poor communication. That is the core of all problems both at work and at home. Margery Kraus with APCO, a global communication consultancy, had this to say on the subject: "Choosing to make effective communication – with employees, investors, clients and in the marketplace – a priority is one of the most important business decisions I ever made. Even the best ideas need to be well articulated. Every entrepreneur needs a communication plan; whether it is a handmade sign in front of a lemonade stand or a multimillion dollar integrated global communication campaign, businesses depend on effective messaging. Companies that succeed take the time to develop a plan to open the right doors, say the right things, and reach the right audiences. Communication is too important to be an afterthought."

Margery continues, "If you are a beginning entrepreneur you might be tempted to put off discussions with potential employees, vendors, maybe even your spouse, preferring to keep things loose. You might even think this is wise under the premise you haven't made any promises. I'll let you know right now that even if words aren't spoken, if people are taking action on your behalf, expectations are set. It is just better to be up front in all you do. I understand that the reason you might not be communicating as much as you should is that you are unclear yourself what to expect. That is understandable with a new venture. Clarity comes from action and discussing what you hope to have happen. People understand, they just don't want to feel taken advantage of even if it is done indirectly and without malice. If you live by the golden rule you will always be ok."

Establishing a strong corporate culture is the best move you can make as a leader. Corporate culture can make or break a company. I experienced this at EarthCare. It is really important to get and keep everyone on board with the process. Employees should feel valued and an integral part of the business, one in which everyone is working as a cohesive team toward a common purpose. An open-door policy empowers people. As CEO, you must be approachable and comfortable with communicating.

The leader needs to have a clear vision of where the company is headed and be able to articulate and motivate others to buy into that vision. Be able to clearly convey the opportunity and growth plan of the company. What people fear most is the unknown.

An effective CEO needs to be seen as committed. Become known for being out in the trenches. Employees love seeing the CEO work as hard as they do! Great CEOs make it comfortable to have an open conversation by bringing others into the discussion and getting their ideas. They are the first to ask a question and the last to speak. They seem to have an innate ability to extract the best from each person.

Tory Johnson, Founder of Women for Hire and *Good Morning America's* Work Place Contributor, offers this customer relations advice, "I used to worry about asking for feedback from clients, assuming that it was giving them permission to complain. I didn't want to know what they had to say because I was so fearful of hearing complaints, or that somebody might have something critical to say about my business. What

I came to recognize is that asking for feedback was a really great way to spot new business development opportunities and a chance to show customers how much we appreciated them by being ultra responsive. For the most part, feedback is an opportunity to get fantastic, free focused group advice from the people who are closest to spending their money with you. It's a really valuable way to learn how you can improve your business, grow your business, and find new opportunities for extensions of products or services that perhaps you hadn't thought of simply by asking. Don't be afraid to ask for feedback."

Tory continues, "Customer service really is number one. It's an overused statement primarily because it is so true! One of the things that everyone on my staff knows is if any complaint is received, I want to know about it – no matter how small or seemingly insignificant. I want to know. I care about complaints equally from the businesses that paid to participate in our events as much as any complaints received from those who attended free of charge. They are giving us a currency that's just as valuable, their time. We have often learned the bark tends to be worse than the bite! Someone will send a really nasty email message about an experience, and we respond. In fact, we reply to every single letter that we receive. Wouldn't you know it, as soon as we answer their message, it's almost as if they do a complete turn-around. They are so impressed we actually care about their complaint. Just by reaching out to respond we have left them with a better impression."

Opportunity

Gloria Mayfield Banks, Executive National Sales Director with Mary Kay and Founder, Charisma Factor, Inc., is a dynamic woman who leads by example. Her opinion is that opportunity falls in our laps all the time, and that we often don't take advantage of it. She says, "A lot of people will spend their time evaluating what they don't have, as opposed to examining what they do have, and acknowledging what gifts and talents make them unique. What can you bring to the table? What of yourself can you give away to others? What impact can you have on the world? These are the things that really will make a difference for women as they build their entrepreneurial careers."

Gloria maintains, "We should play to our strengths rather than to our liabilities. Success comes to those who have figured out how to help enough other people achieve their goals, dreams, and desires. Your weaknesses become less of an obstacle because where you shine becomes so much brighter. I started my life knowing that I wanted to climb the corporate ladder and break the glass ceiling until I found out it was brick. Many people need more flexibility and control. As an entrepreneur, you really do get paid for your efforts. It's a matter of commitment. You have a choice; build a small, medium, or large business. Decide what's right for you and get to it!"

"I have learned how not to be so overwhelmed. I have learned the power of the list and the power of saying no. It's extremely important that you prioritize what's most time-critical, because when you are a doer and you make things happen, everybody wants you to help them. It's great to set big goals if you are willing to parse them down into manageable pieces. You need to be disciplined enough to take a sheet of paper and an ink pen and outline the strategy. Be sure to think it through as far as you can. Remember, it will evolve as you take action and get results."

Setting Expectations

Heidi Roizen, former Silicon Valley Venture Capitalist and Founder of Skinny Songs, reminds us, "When you get rejected there is always another place or another angle, just get up and go do it again."

Lesson number one is you have to be passionate about what you're doing. You have to be driven but you also have to be realistic about how much time you can devote to something and recognize the components of your support system. You need to do your homework. What is different about you? What is your hook? Who is your competition?

Be realistic about what you are trying to accomplish, do your homework, and understand the competition. All the basics of business apply whether you are a one person, sole proprietorship or whether you're planning to start the next Microsoft."

Karen Pearse, Founder of Innovative Stone shares her opinion on business. "I had a vision and pursued it but I think that hard work and luck both played into it. We are a solution-based company and we always look for the solution to what our clients need. A true entrepreneur has a part of her that is a little fearless. If I had listened to fear rather than just going with my gut, I don't think I would be in the place that I am today. I am constantly generating new ideas and solutions for my clients; sometimes it takes a lot to convince them it would really make a difference. That is why it is so important to have a good relationship with them; there must be a great deal of mutual respect and trust in order to get the job done. For me it was really never about the money, it was about feeling successful and meeting challenges.

You don't know what will happen in the future. One has to enjoy the journey along the way. If you find your passion in life and can actually make money at it, what could be better? Finally, how do you reach your potential? It's being true to yourself. No person is an island. Oftentimes reaching your potential means asking others for help. Don't be afraid to ask."

FUNDING

Anne Stanton from Enjoy The City says, "Go to high-net-worth individuals to get started. Once you've brought your business up to a level of viability, then tap into the world of "angels" or venture capital ("VC") when and as needed. You never know unless you ask!"

She VC funded one of her businesses that reached $20 million before going bust during the "dot bomb." Anne learned from her mistakes and has since self funded her new business, a company that is already doing in excess of $10 million and growing. Her suggestion regarding mistakes, "Possessing the ability to bounce back is important. Don't let anybody bring you down, including yourself." Her crisis occurred on a Friday. Instead of giving in or giving up she reopened her doors the following Monday and hasn't looked back since.

Follow your passion, be realistic, and make sure that your business goals fit with your work-life balance. But the first step is to identify a passion and follow it. If you feel at the end of most days that you didn't actually work, i.e. you were doing something you truly enjoy, instead of being engaged in hard labor, then you will be successful because you are following your passion.

Time Realistic

You're trying to build a business and you may even want to become a millionaire from it but more importantly, you want to create your ideal life along the way. The money will come. Once a realistic, valuable business plan that you are passionate about emerges and you have enough hours in a day to dedicate to it, then go for it! The problem I've seen is that there are many moms who start something, but realized once they got into it, that they had only 10 extra hours a week to dedicate to it, not 40 or more.

Natalie Kennedy, Founder of Kennedy Creative: Destination & Event Management offers this advice on gaining customers, "My number one tip is to get face-to-face. Sitting down to a cup of coffee with a client to discuss their goals in person, or taking a meeting with a potential partner can make all the difference. It's about the personal touch. I have made an effort to conduct my business like this from the very beginning, and I feel like it has helped me to form quality relationships with clients, vendors and partners."

Nancy Jane "NJ" Goldston is Founder and Chief Executive Officer of THE UXB™, an award winning, world-class advertising, branding and interactive agency. She had this to say: "Doing great work for clients of THE UXB is a given and part of our culture. I continually remind myself, however, that business success is an ongoing building process based on a strong foundation. I utilize two key strategies which are probably routinely undervalued. First, the importance of growing, maintaining and guarding your cash flow is critical to creating sustainable leverage instead of debt. When combined with slow, controlled growth, versus rapid expansion, you avoid putting undo pressure on yourself and on the business. It's a built-in security blanket when you properly manage your cash flow. You sleep at night.

The other factor that is part of my mantra is "always define your own level of success." Don't let your success be defined by a comparison to someone else's success barometer. If you do, you will always fall short."

Family Support

Typical business books seldom make any reference to family support. Yet, it is a critical component in building a business. With support you will build a stronger business, but more importantly you will build a happier life. Without it, it's an uphill battle and if you do succeed, your family may disintegrate from the lack of communication. Here's what NJ Goldston has to say about her family:

"My twin boys are twenty-one now and they are still affectionate, and my husband and I are still as close as when we first started dating. I really treasure, as a family, that we all emotionally support one another all the time. It gives you a special kind of security every day. Being supportive frees you to be yourself."

Human tendency is to verbally correct what we don't like and largely leave unacknowledged that which we do appreciate. If you want to encourage certain behaviors in your children or your spouse, be sure to reward them with praise when they do it. Praise those people who are important in your life whenever they help you if you want more of the same behavior.

Fran Biderman-Gross, Cofounder of Advantages Printing, Inc., has had a difficult time of it but has persevered and flourished in spite of unexpected tragedy. Her husband died while her two children were young. She knows what it takes to overcome. Her advice is to get a mentor. She says, "It's your business and your baby, but that does not mean you have all the answers. Everyone needs some help and guidance.

A mentor is key to achieving your goals in business. This could be one person to whom you look for advice or a peer group that links many people together who share a common goal."

Employees

Fran recommends building a team that takes pride in their work and wants to succeed. "It's the best investment an owner can make. It makes the day so much easier knowing that you have a group that is out to do their best for the company. The trick is finding the people to fit the business."

"I find the best idea is to give your prospects an evaluation test that shows their strengths, weaknesses, how they work, etc. From there you can see how well they will mesh with everyone else. One thing to keep in mind is to make sure you hire people that complement your work habits/style. Having all of the same type of people working for you leaves a hole in your development. If you are a quiet leader and you hire quiet people under you, you could be missing something since no one will speak up. You need a variety of personalities in the office."

Self Talk

Erika Andersen, Founder of Proteus International, offers one "internal" and one "external" tip, "I think the single most helpful thing I've done in building my success is to become aware of and manage my self-talk. And by that I don't mean doing "affirmations" or "positive thinking." What I'm talking about is recognizing my own personal negative mental monologue – those things I say to myself that aren't helpful – and learning to speak to myself in more productive ways. For instance, some hopeful entrepreneurs (especially women who are trying to be "tough") may say to themselves things like, "It's a dog-eat-dog world out there. I can't trust anyone." Although that self-talk may seem "strong," it's actually counter-productive; it leads you to approach everyone as a potential enemy, thus sabotaging necessary relationships. Instead, they might say to themselves, "Some people are trustworthy and some aren't – I really need to be observant and rely on my experience in deciding who will be good allies."

Listening Skills

Erika continues, "I really believe that skillful and sincere listening is the foundation of success, both in business and personal life. In fact, I'm such a fan of listening that I wrote a whole chapter on it in my first book (and not just any chapter – the first chapter!). Often, when people become managers, and especially when they get to the point where they're running things, they think they're supposed to be the person with all the answers, and they stop listening. I've seen far too many careers derail because executives weren't listening: critical information missed, essential relationships frayed, respect diminished."

Trust your gut

Margery Kraus, President and Chief Executive Officer of APCO Worldwide says, "I always advise clients to "look before you leap" when making business decisions, and I believe that is good advice. But, at the end of the day, you have to trust your instincts. Growing a business involves risk, and striking the right balance between taking risks and maintaining your security – and your sanity – is often the secret of success."

Build a winning team

On building a winning team Margery says, "Don't be afraid to have strong people around you, even if they have more experience than you do. Partners and advisors with a lifetime of success can be a great source of counsel and inspiration. Listen to them, but also be confident in your own abilities and unique contributions. The 'woman factor' should be an asset, not a liability. Women tend to listen more and create a more team-oriented culture. Play to these strengths."

Invest in your reputation

Margery on building reputation, "Businesses today face new and daunting obstacles. Public trust in institutions has been rocked by scandal and disappointment. The demands of a globalized society and 24-hour news cycle challenge companies both small and large. In this skeptical and high-impact culture, intelligent transparency and meaningful corporate responsibility are some of the smartest investments you can make. As you build your reputation and earn your customers' trust, your brand is tangibly strengthened. The conflicting demands on your time, budget, and other resources will always be significant, but doing the right thing – and telling that story effectively – will bring a *Return on Reputation* (ROR) that is always worth the investment."

Think ahead

"Nobody likes to expect the worst," Margery continues, "but everybody should plan for it. When a crisis hits, time is your most valuable resource. Having a basic crisis communication plan ready can mean the difference between weathering a storm and drowning in it. In fact, in many cases it's not the magnitude of the problem, but rather the effectiveness of the response that determines how – and *whether* – a company survives. A strong reputation is your first line of defense against an unforeseen accident, scandal, natural disaster, or product recall. Consumer trust can buy you the time you need to implement your crisis management plan."

Talk to your team

Margery goes on: "Internally focused communication can be as important as external communication. In any business, but particularly those based on ideas, your employees are your most valuable asset. Keeping them informed and inspired is absolutely critical. At APCO, we accomplish this through the publication of regular newsletters, a fully integrated intranet, staff meetings around the world and CEO updates via e-mail or video. We also gather our entire staff for regular global retreats. These meetings are an investment in the company's internal relationships, and the benefits are very real. The interpersonal synergies, new business ideas, and shared vision the meetings engender are invaluable."

Remember to listen

"Communication is a two-way street. Just as it is important to make your voice heard, it is also crucial to listen to what the market is saying. Market research, such as that conducted by APCO's in-house research team, APCO Insight, is the starting point for many of the most successful communication initiatives. It doesn't take an expert to tell you that it is always most effective to focus your communication efforts on the issues that really matter to your audience. Research is the fail-proof way to find out what those issues are."

Be true to yourself

"Take some time to think about your vision for the company," Margery says. "Create a mission statement and make sure that new employees agree to strive for the same goals and uphold the same standards. Not only will your bottom line thank you, you'll also sleep better at night."

Contracts

As a group, women tend to be more trusting then men. That may work well in our personal lives, but in business you will be eaten for lunch if you behave this way. Julie Lenzer Kirk, Founder of Path Forward International, puts it like this, "Trust but verify." We had a large client with whom we had a great relationship and they asked us to develop software for them. Their timeline was such that they did not feel like we had time to negotiate a contract. I wanted to settle the ownership of it before we would move forward and he just kept saying, "Look, just come on, I'll pay you, I'll pay you." I said, "I know you will and

I still want a contract." The thing that saved us was the fact that roughly six months after we convinced him to sign the contract, he died unexpectedly. What would have happened if we had not had this contract? No telling, I mean, it was a multi-million dollar deal. There is no way to speculate on the disastrous impact this would have had on our business had we not had the contract in place."

Partnerships

You should never just spilt things "50/50". Somebody should own 51 percent because otherwise, you are going to get stuck. One partner needs to have the ability to make decisions when the other is not available. Consider setting up a vesting schedule where ownership accrues over time based on milestones being hit. I can tell you from experience there is nothing worse than getting involved with a partner who doesn't do what they are supposed to do. You will end up picking up the slack and they'll be the ones rewarded for your hard work. Don't position yourself badly. Ask your lawyer or CPA for advice in this area.

Intuition

Valerie Fitzgerald, Founder of The Valerie Fitzgerald Group, reminds us to trust our intuition. "I do everything based on how I feel. If it feels right then I know it's right. I think that's one of the biggest tips that I carry with me and live by. I have to go with how I feel about what I am doing. I know that sounds elusive, but it never lets me down. Whenever I go the opposite way of my intuition, it never works out the way I anticipate or intend. A tip for success is to follow your heart."

Action

Tory Johnson, Founder of Women For Hire, discusses building her business. In her words, "Growing the business is really just about cold calling. That's where a background in PR really helped me – just having the confidence to pick up the phone, to recognize that I would get a lot more of no than yes but that I needed to keep plugging way. I knew I had to keep picking up the phone, keep pushing. Here's what I've learned: when you get one "yes," you realize you've found someone who truly values what you have to offer. If you can find one who values it, you could find two and then four and it goes from there. You don't know that unless you are out there doing it. Creating all kinds of charts with forecasts and predictions really doesn't amount to a hill of beans if you can't prove it, if you can't make it happen."

Customer Relations

Julie Lenzer Kirk of Path Forward International offers this advice: "You really have to go out and talk to your customers to validate and shape your business idea to the point it meets a market need. Blogging, getting on discussion boards and just going out and talking to people really help. Talk to whomever you are selling to."

Just Ask

Kristi Frank, from season one of NBC's "The Apprentice" and founder of Saturday Morning Success Series, says, "My advice to people is to just ask for what you need or want. Who cares if they say no! Someone else will say "Yes!" Just put yourself out there and make your needs and desires known."

Marketing

Kristi says, "I do direct mail because a lot of people still like to get something in their mailbox. You may have to send it a couple of times but typically by the third time they will pick up the phone or go on your site just because the flyer is right in front of them, on their desk, waiting for a response."

"I believe in writing articles. My speaking brings in a plethora of customers and contacts. I believe in it all. Showing up in person is really valuable in connecting with people but the Internet is gold."

CANI

"CANI" is an acronym for "constant and never ending improvement." This philosophy is important to consider. Ariana Reed, the millionaire mom of six and network marketer says, "Transform your total life and consistently work on your vocabulary, your mindset, your phrases, the way you run your life, the way you prioritize, the way you are organized. It pays to spend 95 percent of your time leveraging strengths. Write down your top five strengths. I couldn't do that when I first tackled that task, but after some thoughtful reflection, I realized tenacity and loyalty were the top two for me."

I always say I am using tenacity, my loyalty, my aggressiveness to my advantage. Now understand everybody has weaknesses. I have weaknesses that are only too happy to make themselves known! My job is not to stop my weaknesses; it's to minimize the damage. I never focus on my weaknesses. I concentrate on doing what I do well."

"When a sense of peace comes over you and your life feels fulfilled on a much greater level than it has before, you will know it is because you finally feel like the groove fits. It's worth working for!"

Leverage

Most people think of leverage strictly in financial terms. A mortgage is the most widely understood form of leverage. The average person who wants to own a home can do so by putting down a relatively small percentage of the overall cost and financing the rest. The loan allows them to maximize their resources. Many businesses use some form of leverage to finance their venture. It does, however, carry a certain amount of risk. Leverage magnifies both gains and losses.

The term "OPM" or "Other People's Money" is an example of leverage. Investing is often referred to as the balance between fear and greed. My most profitable deals occurred when I followed a plan that included other people's money and investing some of my own.

Somehow knowing I'm using other people's money creates added incentive to do well. After all, if you lose someone else's money they might forgive but they definitely won't forget! The odds of their investing in you again will be slim. For me, knowing I am accountable to others creates an even stronger desire to create value and success for my investors. After all, they believed enough in my abilities to put down their hard earned cash. Be a good steward if the decision is made to go use other people's money. If aren't committed 100% then don't take the money.

Leverage was the reason my environmental start up company had a chance at success. The business plan required millions. The $10,000 of personal investment that I had in clearly wasn't going to cut it. I spent a great deal of time conducting my research and ultimately created a plan, based on a model with a good chance of working. I was able to get investors interested. I had raised $14 million within six months, which was enough to start executing on the business model. Once we saw that our plan was successful, we were able to raise additional funds. Our exit strategy was to take the company public, which we did. Everyone was happy – our investors and our business partners.

Earlier, I referred to real estate as a good example of leverage. At one point, I was approached by a woman with a house problem. She wanted to extricate herself from an awkward situation. Her son and daughter-in-law were living in her old home. She had left and allowed them to move in, paying her $800 per month. The problem was that these people were pigs! We are talking filthy, dirty. As a real estate investor who fixed up old houses, I had seen many dysfunctional households, and this one ranked near the top. The problem, other than the condition of the house, was the woman's relationship with her son. He hadn't been making payments on the house, and he had created a pig sty. She was willing to sell the house at a deep discount to avoid confronting him with an eviction notice and pouring cash into the house in order to make it sellable.

It was May, the month my children get out of school for the summer. I didn't feel like creating additional work for myself. Three boys and long summer days is enough! I did, however, feel badly for her. She obviously loved her son, and he had proved to be a giant disappointment. Here's the leverage proposition I proposed to her: I figured out what the cost to repair the place would be. We took the retail value of the home, subtracted the estimated cost of the necessary repairs, and tacked on profit for a "rehabber" plus a "handling fee" for me. She agreed to the estimate.

The leverage part came when we discussed financing. She ultimately agreed to finance whoever rehabbed the house for three months at $800, the amount her son was supposed to be paying in rent. This was an outstanding deal for a rehabber who typically paid upwards of $10,000 for a deal like this to a hard money lender (meaning very high interest rates for short term loans). It would give this person enough time to fix the house and sell it for $2,400 in holding costs-an outstanding opportunity for the rehabber.

I gave her $10.00 in earnest money to make the deal legit and began marketing the property to investors I knew. Once the terms were realized, I had five candidates lined up within 24 hours to purchase the house in its condition of squalor. I chose someone I knew would keep his commitments. My objective was to make this a win-win for the homeowner, the rehabber, and myself.

All told, it took a month to turn my $10.00 into a $10,000.00. That created 1000 percent cash return on my investment in 30 days. Best of all, everyone involved walked away happy.

What is going to be your form of leverage? Here is a good question to ponder when approaching people to fund your business, "A confused mind always says "no." Effective communication is critical in life, particularly when creating financial leverage. A traditional business plan must clearly outline what is in it for the investor and be thoroughly thought out. It takes clear, effective, and consistent communication to get from concept to reality. The lady in the story above is a great example of this. She was totally on board and then we hit a bump in the road in the form of her brother-in-law, an attorney. Since it was not a typical retail sale, he counseled her to steer clear. In my experience, attorneys play life on defense. Entrepreneurs play offense. The homeowner started waffling.

Before speaking, I listened to her closely. After she was finished I began asking questions. What type of attorney was he? He was a trademark attorney. I acknowledged that selling a house in an optimal situation is confusing and stressful. Creative real estate was an even bigger mystery to most and by default, scarier. Next, I asked her a hypothetical question: if she needed heart surgery, would she consult a kidney doctor? She laughed and said "no." I pointed out that a trademark attorney is not educated on real estate law and therefore his legal advice really didn't apply. He was acting as a concerned family member, which was admirable. The facts remained that her house was a pit and there was a grown man living in it who needed to be evicted. No realtor on earth would agree to list her house. I pulled out my cell phone and wrote down the names of several real estate lawyers with whom I had worked that were familiar with creative real estate transactions. I reminded her I was offering a zero risk, winning solution. The house would remain titled to her until it was sold or refinanced. Worst case scenario – she received free rehab work on her house if the rehabber didn't hold up his end of the bargain. Her son would be removed from the premises (with me as the bad guy), and the house would be fixed up without her spending a dime. She would receive the $800 per month during the three month period, the rent she had initially wanted.

At that point I put the ball in her court. I put a little time pressure on her by reminding her that once my kids got out of school, I would no longer be available. After all, I'd be busy playing at the pool! Whether she called the lawyers I referred I don't know. I did see her body language relax over the course of the discussion. Within 24 hours we were in action mode. Here's the moral of the story: spend the time becoming a creative thinker, a good communicator, and a great listener! It's not about you; it's about your customer.

Sales & Marketing

Let's face it: if the cash register doesn't ring, you don't have a business. It might be a lovely hobby but it's not a business until the cash is flowing. This should cover the debate as to whether you are a salesperson — you are. We all are. The good news is the owner is always the most passionate, so let's put that enthusiasm to work!

If you have the ability to motivate others and deliver real value, your happy customers will become your best salespeople via word of mouth. Referral marketing is the best form of marketing. It's so much better having someone else sing your company's praises!

Fran Binderman Gross from Advantages agrees. She advises other women who are trying to reach her level of success with this, "Referral marketing is the best way to grow your business. Word of mouth business relationships are the strongest. Everyone uses the internet to search for companies that can help them. The problem is finding the right one. It's natural to take one place more seriously than another if that company was recommended by someone you trust. Referrals are unbelievably important in today's world."

She says, "Instead of trying to find unknown people to come to you, prod past customers with whom you have a good rapport to recommend potential clients. These new customers will come in with an idea of what you can do for them already. This makes getting the sale that much easier when the time comes. Your customers will have confidence in you before even speaking with them."

People Endorse What They Help Create

It's helpful to remember the simple phrase above. Think about it... when do you feel most committed to a project? Is it safe to guess, when you are the creator or part of a team? Incorporate this philosophy into everything that goes on within your business. If you do, you'll find loyal, raving fans! How do you do this? Let your imagination run wild. Market research questions (sent via email using free survey templates from sites like Survey Monkey), blogging, and social media are three good places to start.

Drip Method

The key ingredient in sales is persistence. Accept upfront that you will more often than not need to call your targets repeatedly until they either say "yes" or cry "mercy!" If you want to learn to sell, hang around a kindergartner. Children are born salespeople. We should follow their lead. A five year old may look innocent and charming, but underneath lurks a bulldog of a salesperson! If entrepreneurs incorporated only one third of a child's relentless pursuit of the latest Nerf gun or LEGO set, we'd all be billionaires! Here are some interesting sales statistics to soak in:

44% of all salespeople quit after the 1st call

24% quit after the 2nd call

14% quit after the 3rd call

12% quit after the 4th call

= 94% quit after the 4th call

BUT

60% of ALL sales are made after the 4th call.

This means that 94 percent of all salespeople don't give themselves a chance at 60 percent of the prospective buyers!

Female Sales Advantage

There are dozens of books out there on the "how to" of selling that will take a much deeper look at the art of selling. We will, however, touch on a few basics. As women, we have natural sales abilities we can use to our advantage. We are intuitive and we are relationship driven. This gives us a leg up in selling our products and services. Women are adept at reading facial expressions, picking up on variations in vocal tones and body language. This is why, whenever possible, negotiating face to face will work in our favor.

Selling is one of those areas about which people generally have strong opinions. It's either exciting or torturous depending on your attitude. The fact is we are constantly selling. Life is one big negotiation.

Do you find it a struggle to pick up the phone and dial a prospect? Take the focus off of yourself and place it elsewhere. Think about how you are going to be able to help the person on the other end of the line. Think about your children and how you want to be able to provide them with what they need. This will go a long way towards getting you over your fear. Still experiencing it? Well it's time to put on your "big girl pants" and do it anyway!

Remember, selling at the end of the day is a numbers game. It doesn't hurt to think of it this way either. A salesperson's mantra is, "I must do the most productive thing possible at every moment." Time is truly money.

Make sure you amp up your attitude. On a scale of one to 10, you need to be at least an eight when you talk to a prospect. Enthusiasm is contagious. Stand up and swing your arms or jump around. Find little activities that will help you get into an appropriate frame of mind. It never hurts to model others in your field who are already successful. What do they do that seems to be working? Emulate then grow from there.

Remember, everyone is thinking all the time "WIFM" (what's in it for me?). Be sure to answer that question as quickly as you can and as often as necessary to hold your prospect's attention. It pays to know who your customers are, why they buy, and where they are located. It also helps to consider the intangible benefits your product or service offers and sell those as well.

First Impressions

According to Michelle T. Sterling, AICI Principal and Founder of Global Image Group, "Within only the first three seconds of a new encounter, you make an indelible impression. In essence you are evaluated…even if it is just a glance." People appraise your visual and behavioral appearance from head to toe. They observe your demeanor, mannerisms and body language and even assess your grooming and accessories – watch, handbag, and briefcase. This first impression process occurs in every new situation. Within the first few seconds, people pass judgment on you – looking for common surface clues. Once the first impression is made, it is virtually irreversible. It may not seem fair but it's the way of the world. Be aware of what your clothes, make up and hair say about you.

The process works like this:

- If you appear to be of comparable business or social level to the person with whom you're meeting, you are considered suitable for further interaction.
- If you appear to be of higher business or social status, you are admired and cultivated as a valuable contact.
- If you appear to be of lower business or social standing, you are tolerated but kept at arm's length.
- If you are in an interview situation, you can decide whether to match the corporate culture. Keep in mind that your decision may ultimately affect the outcome.

It is human nature to constantly make these appraisals, in both business and social environments. You may have hardly spoken a word, yet once this three-second evaluation is over, the content of your speech will not change it. When you make the best possible first impression, you have your audience in the palm of your hand. When you make a poor first impression, you lose your audience's attention, no matter how hard you scramble to recover it.

You can learn to make a positive and lasting first impression, modify it to suit any situation, and come out a winner. Doing so requires you to assess and identify your personality, physical appearance, lifestyle, and goals. Those who do will have the advantage. Success comes to those with integrity, who are resourceful, and those who make a fabulous impression!

Testimonials

The easiest way to sell something is to have other customers singing your praises. Incorporate satisfied customers into your selling. A video testimonial is the most powerful. It can be incorporated on the home page of the company website or even put into power point presentations.

Rapport

I've stated this before, but it is so important, that it bears repeating. You have two ears and one mouth. Be sure to use them in that order when working with a prospective client. Build rapport first, understand the prospect's needs and desires, than show how your product or service solves their problem. Craft each presentation to address that person's particular needs. They don't want to hear every single thing you have to say; they only want to know specifically how your product handles their concerns. Ask lots and lots of questions.

Once you've built a trusting rapport with a prospect, your next job is to show how your product or service solves their problems. There are "situation" questions and "meaning" questions. Situation questions concern the customer's current situation in the area of your product or service. For example, what product or service is the customer using now? Is the customer satisfied? The key is not to accept the surface answers. For example, if the prospect says, "We're satisfied with our current supplier," you answer, "Your current supplier is an excellent organization. But we have a different approach that is getting better results. Let me show you."

Meaning questions are used to pinpoint exactly how a problem affects the customer. For example, you could ask questions such as, "What does the problem mean to you? How much is it costing you? What indirect costs are affected?" Meaning questions help you uncover the full consequences of a problem.

In your sales presentation, you can then emphasize the full consequence of buying your product. People do things for one reason – to be better off after the action. Your job as a salesperson is to convince buyers that they will be better off after they have purchased your product or service.

All buying is emotional because people are emotional in everything they say or do. The final purchase decision will be strongly influenced by emotional reasons. I'm sure you've heard the term "hot button." The hot button is the most highly emotional reason for purchasing. It's usually related to the respect and esteem of other people. Well-targeted hypothetical questions can uncover the hot button. The customer's answers are also hypothetical, but they can give you the key benefit you have to address to make the sale.

For example, the next time you're looking for a prospect's hot button you might ask one of these questions, "If you were ever to buy this product, what would you want it to do for you? "What would you absolutely have to be convinced of in order to purchase this product or service?"

Look at your product or service. What does it do for the customer? That's what you should concentrate on in your sales presentation. If you do this, be prepared for loads of new business!

Remember, selling is about competence, clarity, and communication. Help others have confidence in your business by clarifying and communicating how you will take away the client's pain with the benefits of your product or service.

Fund Raising

Here's the down low from my experience raising $60 plus million dollars for my business ventures in three distinct industries having bought and/or sold thirty businesses and pieces of real estate. The short answer is that there is always money available for the right idea at the right time.

The trick is getting in front of the right people and not getting discouraged when you hear "no" a bunch of times (especially in this market). Raising capital is a sales function which means it's a numbers game. Karen Rands, founder of Kugarand Holdings and NBAI, touted by Inc. Magazine as one of the nation's top seventy five angel investment groups, gives this piece of advice, "Angel investors typically will put in $25,000 to $50,000 on average. For every check writer you will have three that you think will invest and a total of fifteen that will look at your business plan."

Another tip is to share your milestones with those who can help you. If an investor sees you making progress over time, the odds of his interest in investing in your company increase. Remember, it's the jockey people bet on, not the horse. My preference has been to talk with investors within the industry in which I am operating. Then half the battle is half won already. They get it. I just have to be convincing, so the management team can see by looking at the business plan what's in it for them.

I have always raised funds in a way that flows with the current economic cycle rather than against it. When IPOs were hot, I structured my business model from the start to take advantage of the trend. When I was active in real estate, I leveraged OPM (other people's money). In today's marketplace it pays to experiment with creative financing methods also known as bootstrapping.

Bootstrapping is an approach where the entrepreneur spends as little money as possible to launch his/her venture quickly to see if the market exists for their product. Bartering services is an example of bootstrapping. It's maximizing every dollar that you lay out for your business. It has become more difficult and time consuming to find large amounts of capital for new entrepreneurs and unproven products or services. However, this is no reason not to start your company now. With additional talent readily available, the time is perfect for new and adaptable companies to step in and thrive.

Bootstrapping allows for an entrepreneur to start a business without having to put themselves in a tremendous amount of debt and keeps them from giving up too much equity.

My current venture – www.millionairemoms.com – offers a wealth of information. I have asked these successful moms how they raised their funds. The answers have been fascinating. Women typically take a different approach from that of men towards raising money. They tend to want to self fund more than their male counterparts and don't typically consider venture capital funding at all.

Here are two examples of creative financing I've run across. One mom sent her business plan package to 30 CPAs. She figured they'd know which of their clients would have an appetite for her type of investment. She sent a letter asking they review the plan and submit it to clients who might be interested. She followed up with the accountants and got her project funded. A member of millionairemoms.com heard this idea and did the same thing. She got funded as well.

Yet another successful mom told me how she enlisted her local university to help her write her business plan. I thought this was a good idea. I tried it and it worked. The MBA students took on my project.

Universities put on business plan competitions each year. The cash prize money is substantial ranging from $10,000 to $100,000 per competition. This is significant seed money to grow a business. Venture capitalists are the judges. They give feedback to each company in the competition. What a wonderful networking opportunity! It is also great at helping you polish the pitch on your business plan power point if you plan to seek outside funding.

This isn't for everyone but the point is, think outside the "have to get a bank loan" box. There is more than one way to skin a cat!

If you want additional boot strap insider secrets from other entrepreneurs on how they funded their businesses with tight budgets, then sign up for my free weekly eZine at our website www.millionairemoms.com and get this valuable eBook as our complimentary gift. It is very inspiring!

Here is what Kayla Fioravanti, Founder of Essential Oils, had to share about her experience growing her company: "We started by operating out of our kitchen. We had no money and no ability to get a loan. We decided to become the company that worked with small companies. We started producing in bulk and offered really low minimums or no minimum to order. This helped other small businesses get up and running; many of them were stay-at- home moms just starting out. That was a missing niche. It was crazy…we posted a company website that we got in a box for $30 and put all our information on the front page. From that, everyone just assumed we were really big yet we were still operating out of our kitchen. We moved from there to 600 square feet to 2,500 square feet and currently occupy close to 30,000 square feet. We've used the power of the Internet; we started marketing to everything that we could that was free or less than $10. So we started working on "spidering" and giving -- we never used Google ads or anything like that, we just hooked up with other people in the industry. There is an organization called The Indie Beauty Network that helped us with marketing our business. We just kind of ended up spreading the word about the industry ourselves."

Nancy Bogart, Founder of Jordan Essentials, said she funded her company one penny at a time! "We used a traditional bank for a loan, but as a direct sales company, we often face discrimination when we ask for lending. I'm not sure why, but the prejudice is there and being a woman owner of a direct sales company, I felt that I was fighting a particularly tough battle. Fortunately, it was nothing that my spiritual faith and a little moxie couldn't help me overcome. No matter your need, never assume the worst; always assume the best in people and your situations. There is a solution; you just have to find it. Cash flow has always been and continues to be one of our biggest hurdles regardless of the size of our company."

Annie Stanton, Founder of Enjoy The City, suggests, " Go to high-net-worth individuals to get started and once you get your business up to a certain point that you have a proven, viable business model, then tap into the angel or venture capital world when and as needed. You never know unless you ask!" She continues, "If you do a deal, walk away knowing in a liquidity event, you might not see another penny and all the rest is gravy. If you are okay with that, then do the deal."

There is much to consider in starting and growing a business. The good news is that you don't have to accomplish everything at once. It is worth noting that you don't have to fully understand all these different types of funding in order to get started. When I began I had no idea what a "private placement memorandum" was. I learned as I needed to. The objective is to break the overall business plan into manageable daily tasks. Remember the Chinese proverb, "When is the best time to have plant a tree? The answer: twenty years ago. When is the second best time to plant a tree? The answer: Today." Get out there, plant some trees, and get busy creating your ideal life!

Business Advice

THOUGHT GENERATOR

If you think taking a risk is scary, then consider the alternative. Where will you end up if you DON'T take a risk? That can be a bigger fear than not trying!

Write your thoughts here:

_____

_____

_____

_____

_____

_____

_____

_____

CHAPTER SIX

What I Wish I Knew Then That I Know Now

by Margery Kraus, President and CEO, APCO Worldwide
www.apcoworldwide.com

If only crystal balls really worked! I probably would have been a bit startled to see what predictions mine held. As a first generation American, I shared my parents' belief that things come to people who work hard. My mother's constant theme was that where there is a will, there is a way. Little did I realize how true it was! Of course, luck and timing have a lot to do with it as well.

Today, I am fortunate to run a business that I created 25 years ago. I have close to 600 wonderful employees who make my company a special place – a place where we help our clients solve their problems and leverage their opportunities through effective communication with their many stakeholder audiences. Little did I know when I started that the company would be so successful.

I am often asked what I learned along the way. Here are a few of the most important lessons:

1. **Never look back.** I have had to make many choices in this journey, including leaving another job I loved to take on the assignment of starting APCO. At each juncture, I agonized over the decisions I had to make. These decisions seemed overwhelming at the time, but in retrospect, I went with my gut and tried not to second-guess myself. I am sure there are some things I would have done differently, but once

you make a decision, be comfortable with it. There is nothing to be gained by looking back.

2. **Do a good job at whatever you are doing.** When I began my career, having a five-year plan was in vogue. I never had one. In retrospect, having a plan would have limited my choices. I think that you have to take things on, do the best you can at what you tackle and see where it leads. Don't over-plan your life. Be flexible and take chances.

3. **It is amazing what you learn from motherhood.** There is a lot to be said for learning the skills of being a good parent. What is interesting is how many of those skills also make you a good leader and mentor. Just as you build a sense of well-being for your children and help them build a sense of efficacy, the same skills are needed to grow and mentor a staff. I think women have great advantages in their leadership and management skills because of the experience of motherhood. It makes us more "tuned in." Despite the fact that society seems to discount much of that experience, we should embrace it and utilize it in other life experiences.

4. **Having a good family life and a supportive spouse will help lead to success.** Just as you cannot build a business without the cooperation of a good team, your team on the home front must back you as well. Having a spouse who delights in your success and is honest when you need to hear unpleasant things is an essential ingredient to being a balanced professional. I am also fortunate to have three wonderful children, now all married with their own lives, who were my cheerleaders, my helpmates and, yes, an occasional cause of distress, but who supported me in every key professional decision I made. I learned a lot from them and still do.

5. **Guilt is overrated.** Early in my career, I spent a lot of time feeling guilty. I was worried about time away from my family. I was worried I couldn't be as active in school for my kids. I was worried about everything. As my kids got older, I realized that quality, not quantity was important. Communication was essential. I also found that giving

them responsibility for their own lives was a great gift. I now have the pleasure of watching them pass this gift on to their children.

6. **Don't become reliant on the so-called "experts."** I don't know if it is a female trait or a function of inexperience, but I always felt I didn't have the expertise in one or more particular areas. While getting advice and listening is important, don't sell yourself short. You may be closer to the situation and have a better feel for what is possible than you think. Seek advice and counsel, listen and learn, but don't delegate important decisions based upon expert advice. Have the confidence to rely on your own judgment.

7. **Think big and have passion.** Life is too short for small dreams. If you believe in what you do, think big. Passion can fuel a lot of big dreams. Most of all, when life gets overwhelming, make lists. Know yourself and what you can do well. Rely on everyone else for the other things. When life gets you down, find those things that make you happy and renew your spirit…and then move on to the next thing on the list!

What I Wish I Knew Then That I Know Now

by Nancy Bogart CEO, Jordan Essentials bath, body and spa
www.jordanessentials.com

In the fall of 1999, the voice of need kept calling me back into the work place. Ok, so it really sounded a lot like my husband Ron. We had three young kids at the time, bills were mounting and I had been fortunate enough to be able to stay at home for six years. Every family comes to major crossroads of decisions and many times we use the element of reality or fear to dictate our choices. Looking back, I am actually glad I did not know everything to come and yet I would have loved to have started our company with some experience…any experience.

I began to use my strengths to make a game plan. I wanted to generate an income without having to actually take on a job. My background and degree were in Hotel and Restaurant Management, specializing in catering and party planning. I loved to create recipes and, in the years prior to having children, I enjoyed a successful catering business, but the hours were just crummy. I think everyone should lean on their strengths; there is no point in being someone you are not just to make a buck. I wanted more than just the career I had before the kids were born. I wanted it all: the hours, flexibility, fun and money. I had been participating in a few craft fairs for extra money for the holidays and now it was time to turn up the heat before Ron did. I spent a few long hours reading, praying and looking for an answer. I came across a book about how the pioneer women made their own lotions and soaps. I loved the idea of cooking without the food ingredients. Pioneer women used bars made from fats and oils poured into bars. My grandmother had solid perfume and the idea grew from there. I bought my supplies using beeswax as a base and fabulous oils and made my own unique bar of lotion.

We ultimately sold almost one million of these in eight years. We incorporated into a direct sales company much like the Pampered Chef and Tupperware. More than 8000 women across the country in all 50 states, Guam and Puerto Rico would sell all of those one million bars in a special partnership to help their families; and I would never have to have that "job." I would support and them and train them on how to plan house parties in order to share our now full line of products women love and can afford.

Trust your instincts.

Too often in the early years I thought I was so inexperienced and that everyone else around me had better ideas and knew more; therefore, I often deferred the decision making to others. I would think, "Well, I am just a mom; what do I know?" I started this company without ever having used a cell phone, possessing no computer skills and having stayed home for six years. It was my dream, so I simply took it one step at a time. Use your God given strengths and be ok to learn new things without ever putting yourself down along the way. Be a life long learner and enjoy the journey.

Not everyone will love the dream like you do.

If this is your dream, and you are the owner, you really do care more than anyone else. It never occurred to me people who were with me in the beginning would ever leave. Of course, we do have many long time friends and consultants still with us, however, the number who left is far greater. I had to get better at the release. It is not everyone's life purpose to be in our company for all time . There are seasons in life and ways of life. A season of life is temporary and short term. A way of life is confidence, strength, purpose and vision. As much as I adore my family, they have their own lives, too, and it was only for a season during which they were an active part of our company. Seasons in life come and go – be sure to keep the most important thing which is Love. Nothing is greater than love and being loving to someone as they end a season with you. You never know when a new season with that person might start. A good friend once told me to have a revolving door on your business and life. Let people come and go, and you will have an abundance of people in your life.

We all need rest. If I ever looked back at the hours I spent cultivating the business, and then put that up against my paycheck, I would probably lose my mind. Passion has more benefits than just pay. Look for the benefits of friends and spend time with them. What is the point when your company is on the top 100 list and you haven't got a friend to your name and you have to put nametags on your kids because you forgot their names? This is a nasty trap into which many of us fall. We do not think our time counts because we will be here no matter what. Get out of the building and schedule family time first. There will be seasons of sacrifice but do not make it a way of life. The future is really yours.

There is no place for doubt about your bright future. You might have a bump in the road or two, but ultimately, your future is your choice. I was taught a long time ago that a dream is something you create, nurture and grow into reality. Only *you* can give up that dream. Through the difficult seasons of my career (and there have been many) it would have been easier to throw up my hands and quit until I remembered my dream – to help women keep their faith and family first while making a good part time or lucrative full time income selling our high quality bath and body products.

What I Wish I Knew Then That I Know Now

by Farah Perelmuter, Co-Founder, Speakers' Spotlight
www.speakers.ca

I was always a "visionary." Well that's not exactly the term my friends used when describing me. I remember clearly one day having a discussion with my friend and her explaining to me, "Farah, there is always one thing in a person that makes him or her crazy. For you, it's being a dreamer." A *dreamer*? But that insinuates that my big plans were never going to actually materialize. What my friend didn't realize was that I was working hard to make sure they did. I actually had already come a very long way.

I always "saw" my future. When I was a teenager growing up in Winnipeg, Manitoba (Canada), I pictured myself owning a glamorous business (a modeling agency perhaps?) and working out of a fabulous space. The elevator would open directly onto my floor (my agency occupied the entire floor), I would have a glass desk and a view of the CN tower. Well, I knew that to make this happen I had to move to Toronto (that's where the CN tower is). As soon as I graduated high school, I packed my bags and at the age of 17 my adventure began.

After many years of post-secondary education in Ontario, a brief career in advertising, I eventually met my future husband Martin, and together, we decided to quit our jobs and start our own business, Speakers' Spotlight (www.speakers.ca). We, and our staff across Canada, represent and book the most fascinating personalities to speak at events worldwide. We represent everyone from former and prospective Canadian Prime Ministers, to astronauts and Mount Everest climbers, international best-selling authors to world acclaimed comedians, leading-edge business thinkers, celebrities and the most inspiring individuals. After 13 years and occupying six different venues, our head office in Toronto can now be found just off the elevator on its own floor, and you will find me at my glass desk and behind me, through the window, you will see a view of the CN Tower.

I "saw" everything I wanted. From where I worked, to what I wore (I eventually crossed shoulder pads off my list) to what I wanted to do (Speakers' Spotlight was originally based on how a modeling agency operated but instead of selling beauty, we provide ideas and inspiration). I wasn't "dreaming," I was "visioning." And I thought I saw it all. But suddenly my world changed on September 12, 2000 and I realized I didn't have a clue. Her name is Jade.

My whole life I knew I wanted to be a mother more than anything else. I saw myself being a mommy with a baby on one hip and another playing at my feet. We would dance and do arts and crafts, go to the park and use our imaginations all day long. I've always been excited for that scene in my life. Although constantly dreaming of career success, having a family had always been my top priority.

Now Jade is eight and our son, Cole, is six. The one thing I have realized in recent years is that I had never visualized having that idyllic family scene and that high-powered career scene *at the same time.* I never saw what a successful businesswoman's life would look like while being a wonderful wife and a fantastic mother to young children. And I thought I was so prepared for my future!

So, here I am. Speakers' Spotlight has succeeded well beyond what Martin and I could have ever imagined. We have won awards, are often asked to speak to entrepreneurs and have been written up in various books and media worldwide, even a business textbook. That kid in Winnipeg would be shocked. Our two little ones are thriving too. We believe they are growing up to be conscientious, kind people. At least, as their parents, that is what we are striving to teach them. And for me? I have to admit, it's a constant, difficult tug-of-war. Wanting to be at the office every day with my staff (and feeling I should be there) and wanting to be with my kids every day after school (and feeling I should be there) is not easy for me. I know that many mothers can relate to that. It's tough. Balancing one's career, one's family, and actually finding time for oneself can be overwhelming.

For me, my family scene still comes first. So even though my husband hears me quietly grumbling about my carpools and how I have to rush from work to pick up the kids, I want to be there to take them home. I want to be there to help with homework and story time. I've had to miss some exciting events and fabulous parties over the years, but all those snuggles at bedtime make up for it. It hasn't been easy, and I'm still in the thick of it trying to figure it all out, but I know one day Jade and Cole won't need me to drive them home from school, or to help them with arts and crafts. I guess we won't be dancing around the living room forever… I know I need to do that now. They will one day be all grown up and I never want to regret not spending time with them…while they still want me to. My career will continue, perhaps not as robust and full as it could be, and one day will be, but it's a choice that I'm so fortunate I can make. I just can't have it all right now. But then again, maybe I do.

I'm lucky, and I've worked hard. I pictured exactly what I wanted and have actually achieved both my visions. One day our children will take over the business and Martin and I will reminisce about these times while traveling around the world, stopping to rent a villa high atop a mountain with a view of the ocean, drinking tea watching the sun set…Well, I can *dream*, can't I?

What I Wish I Knew Then That I Know Now

by Sandra Yancey, Founder & CEO, eWomenNetwork.com
www.ewomennetwork.com

One of the greatest secrets to success is to understand the power of your network. Make no mistake about it; everyone who succeeds has a network. It is no surprise to realize that much of what you learn today will quickly become obsolete. Technology and business are changing and evolving so rapidly. We simply cannot learn what we need to know fast enough to keep up with the whirlwind of changes we face each and every day. Here's the good news: it's OK. You will find that the success of your future has more to do with knowing "who" versus knowing "how." That's right. Powerful people are no longer defined by their fancy titles, expensive clothes or corner offices. Rather, powerful people are defined by their ability to make things happen and get things done, both for themselves and others.

Your network should be built on the foundation of some key constituents. The earlier you identify and build a solid relationship with them, the more stable and sustaining your network will be. Take inventory of your relationships now and be sure you can identify one mentor whose role is to provide you "access"; two role models—people you admire and wish to emulate; and three connectors—people who easily and willingly connect people to other people. Each one of these constituents will play a unique and important role in your continued growth and development.

To establish a growing and evolving relationship with your core constituents, you must first recognize, believe and behave according to the philosophy of "*It takes teamwork to make the dream work.*" It is through the spirit of abundance that you first demonstrate your own character and integrity of helping others. After all, how can you expect others to do for you what you are not first willing to do for them? The point here is, powerful networkers believe in "giving first." They constantly and consistently look for ways to share contacts, resources, information and leads without the expectation of anything in return. They live the law of the universe; that is, you must give in order to receive. And, you inherently know that when you give freely and without expectations, you will be rewarded ten-fold.

Savvy networkers show up! They put their face in the place; they are seen in the scene. They are attentive and alert wherever they go, whether it is a business function or the dry cleaners. They always wear a smile (the only universal language) and generate conversation. They ask great questions and listen more than speak. They always try to leave a conversation with the gift of a lead handwritten on the back of their business card. They know that through helping others, they are helping themselves, and by helping themselves, they can repeat the cycle. In the end, success is not about ME; it's about WE. It really does take teamwork to make the dream work. I wish you the best of luck in all you do. Just remember, "Give first, share always."

What I Wish I Knew Then That I Know Now

by Nadja Piatka, Founder, Nadja Foods
www.nadjafoods.com

The Strength of a Woman

I grew up in a household where the man was boss. Even though my mother worked side by side with Dad in the family business, it was my father who made the major decisions. For my family, it was a cultural and generational trend of the times. As much as I believed that my new generation of women would do better, I grew up, married and became a "gosh and golly, please and thank you" wife. When after almost 20 years of marriage, my husband came home to tell me he was leaving me for someone else; I became the head of my own household comprised of two children and myself. After a lifetime of deferring to men, I found myself in a position for which I had no training.

As a result of my ex-husband's financial problems, I had to move my children out of our big beautiful home to a much smaller one. When we first walked into our new house, my son said, "Are our friends going to laugh at us when they see where we live?" Things went from bad to worse, and our terrible luck seemed never-ending. The day I made my daughter hide under the table with me from a bill collector, I felt I had hit rock bottom. At that moment, I went from a fetal position of defeat to a desire not only to survive for my children, but to thrive.

Every small accomplishment reinforced my strength and belief in me and I loved the transformation. I like who I have become and so do my children...Or maybe, like my mother, it's who I always was but never let it show. I truly believe that strength is in every one of us. One of my favorite sayings is by Thomas Edison: "If you did all the things in life that you are truly capable of, you would literally astound yourself."

What I Wish I Knew Then That I Know Now

by Cordia Harrington, Founder, CEO, President,
Tennessee Bun Company
www.thebuncompany.com

Being an eternal optimist—and one who sees every problem as an opportunity—I do not think backwards. So I will try to tell you what has been a steady theme in my life—what has worked, and what hasn't.

1. ***Rushing through life causes problems!*** Being in a hurry, being more "efficient" when working with people, does not work out. Most relationships and business deals take time and cannot be rushed. I think being in a hurry makes others feel uncomfortable and unappreciated, so now I try to think about how being rushed feels to others. I try to take it more slowly, giving time for an idea to percolate and a problem to be worked out. In the bakery, the yeast takes four full hours to make the dough rise, and you cannot rush it. Taking time to let issues resolve, to get problems solved and to let relationships develop is important to know!

2. ***Get out of your comfort zone*** — learning every position in the company is important! From working shoulder to shoulder with them, you will engender admiration from your team. They will respect that you know what they are doing—that you are not too good to do their jobs and that you are equal to them, with everyone having an important role. When we know all the roles in the company, we can see at a glance that things are being done correctly; we can praise good works and correct problems more quickly.

   I've read that to become a McDonald's franchisee, an applicant must first devote 2,200 hours to working in a

McDonald's restaurant. This gives prospective franchisee an opportunity to know every detail of the restaurant, and it gives McDonald's a chance to see if the person has the personality, temperament and passion to be successful. I think this practice should be carried to every profession!

3. ***Saving early pays off big time!*** There is magic in compound interest—if you can save $10 every month in the early years, it can grow and double. For instance, if you can put aside $1,200 for your unborn child, when he or she is 65, that $1,200 will be $97,500. And if you start saving $75 a month for life, it can turn into $1,194,975 at 7 percent interest, or $3.4 million at 9 percent interest! Start when the child is born, then let them take over the saving every month when they are old enough to contribute—it really adds up! When my three sons were born, I saved $1200 and purchased zero coupon bonds—it was $20,000 by the time they got ready to attend college. It wasn't enough to cover the total bill, but it sure did help!

4. ***Have passion about your career and your place!*** Loving what you do will energize you to be wildly successful! Whatever your passion, you can be successful if you give 100 percent. You may have passion for the outdoors during college and graduate with a degree in landscape architecture. But over time, your passion may change, and that is ok! Follow your passion, even if it changes. Let the place where you are influence your soul!

Think about the people you deal with: those who are passionate are the most fun to do business with. They are the ones we return to time and again. I am known as the "Bun Lady," and I love what I do. I have a funny title, but it opens doors for me to share that we make over 1,000 buns every minute and serve some of the most elite customers in the world. I am passionate and enthusiastic about my career choice!

What I Wish I Knew Then That I Know Now

by Nancy Jane (NJ) Goldston, Founder and CEO, The UXB

www.theuxb.com

Your Career Is An Ongoing Process. It Never Ends. It Just Changes.
Like the majority of working mothers, I felt quite conflicted. I sang the mantra we all sing to each other about being exhausted. "I'm juggling my family, juggling my job and I am looking for a way to have it all." I seemed to be doing it exceedingly well and moving up the corporate ladder at a rapid pace but feeling guilty most of the time. And that's when I started to think about how I would leave my big corporate life and start to balance family and work. Be with my kids. Be more available for my husband. Perhaps feel a little less stressed and get back to doing what I love. Be creative. Become the master of my schedule and my life. Leave the safe and secure corporate nest.

On my way to this other life, I had to give up the prestige of having a big corporate job; my identity was securely attached to being a successful executive who hands out impressive business cards and I needed to confront some real "truths". Did I have a "go to war" skill? Yes, *I am strategically creative*. Did it have real value in the market place? Yes. Could I engineer my own success without the power and backing of a large enterprise? Yes. Could I (and this was the BIG question) be a rainmaker? Could I stand on my own two feet? Would anyone listen to me? Think I was an expert? Could I make money? Yes, yes, yes and yes.

So the corporate ending became a new beginning. I transitioned. Felt a bit lonely. No, very lonely. It's hard being on your own without a support system. I reflected on my many mistakes in my corporate career and I can happily catalog them now. I took too many things personally. I should have given my bosses more credit. I should have thought a bit more before reacting to certain situations. But, I catalogued my achievements too. I am extraordinarily industrious, a team leader and most of all an experienced marketing and creative professional who has built a wonderful network. I hung my advertising agency shingle out and got to work.

I became ever accommodating and ever changing as I slowly built my business. I talked about my vision to anyone and everyone who would listen. I was inclusive and most of all, I kept evolving and creating a larger vision over time. Each success led to more success but the way *I* wanted to define it. I moved away from that large corporation that was my home. I got back to the real work and away from the politics. I cared about the clients, brought my passion and dedication to their companies and in the process, everyone at the agency succeeded because we were (and are) a passionate team. I gained the freedom to choose how I work and with whom, as well as who I hired. In the process, I found myself, experienced a fuller family life, surrounded myself with a team that inspires me every day and built a business. Most importantly, I redefined my own level of success. It never ends. It just changes.

What I Wish I Knew Then That I Know Now

by Karen Pearse, CEO and President, Innovative Stone
www.innovativestone.com

Don't Throw Your Vision Out with the Bath Water

I've always loved stories about people who have achieved great things by sticking to a vision. Michael Phelps swam into the history books at the Olympics, after applying a single minded, bent-on-winning approach to training. Oprah Winfrey continues to out-entrepreneur us all with her branded media empire and socially responsible charities. Barak Obama stuck to a message and a plan, refused to be distracted by pundits, naysayers and competitors, and won the presidential election. Those stories are inspirational. More importantly, they help simplify the extraordinarily complicated world in which we live. Have a clear vision. Stick to it. Avoid distraction. You'll achieve your goals.

I don't think you can start a business and make it a successful enterprise without a clear vision backed by passion. Starting and running a business is exhausting work filled with difficult decisions – How should the company be financed? How much leverage is too much leverage? When should we hire the marketing manager? What are we going to do about the new hire who isn't working out so well? Just to name a few. You can't head to work every morning and face those decisions if you're not toting along passion for a vision.

I'm extremely vision driven. Before I had an idea of what I wanted to do, I had a clear vision of what I *didn't* want to do. I didn't want to work for someone else. My father had always owned his own business so my entrepreneurial spirit is partly genetic, but only partly. I've always felt less vulnerable when I was in charge of what was happening in my work life. It's naïve to think that we're ever completely in charge of the businesses we run. The economy is out there doing things, we have managers making day to day decisions, and our customers and partners certainly throw curves every now and again. I know I can't control *everything* but I like controlling what I can.

After working for other people for several years, I developed a vision for what I *did* want to do – a business that I wanted to start and build. I've always loved beautiful things, certainly not an uncommon preference. How many people *don't* love beautiful things? I'm compelled by natural things that last for generations that are of high quality, that are durable, and that go a long way towards making aesthetic improvement. I focused on stone, specifically granite and marble. My vision was simple: a profitable company, solely-owned by me, that sourced stone building products to the commercial market.

In 1981, I started Innovative Tile and Stone. By 2000, we had grown a small business to one that employed 36 people and worked with renowned architects. We specified and sourced stone for buildings like the MGM Grand Hotel and Casino in Las Vegas, the Time-Warner building in Manhattan, and the Palace of the Lost City in South Africa. We also had contracts to supply materials for Macy's, Saks Fifth Avenue, Nordstrom and Bloomingdale's projects across the country.

Things were good. Innovative was successful by any measure. Our staff was tight and motivated. (We hosted fun events like the Innovative Olympics in my family's backyard). Businesses grow or die, and we knew that we couldn't simply rest on our laurels if we wanted to be successful. Our entrenchment in the commercial building market left us vulnerable to uncontrollable swings in that sector. And because our business was heavily skewed to a few key partners, our fate was inextricably tied to theirs. I thought it was time for a new vision.

I gathered Innovative Stone's key managers and some outside friends and debated on moves that would help us diversify. Several alternatives were considered. We could move into the mausoleum and tombstone market. It's a bit morose but there's a niche that isn't going to go away. Market consistency is appealing but mausoleums and tombstones didn't seem like fun. We looked at opening markets in other countries;

leveraging our expertise and partnerships to broaden the commercial market and lessen the impact of downturns in any particular geography. That was certainly doable but it didn't sing to us.

We settled on the revelation that was the most challenging but potentially the most lucrative. We decided to enter the retail market – stone products for the home – and build a national brand. A brand is security, a hedge against economic downturns. No one could take the brand away from us, and we could apply it to a broader range of products over time. A brand would help us maintain control of Innovative while growing the company.

Of course, building a brand is both time-consuming and expensive. Innovative Stone's cash position was strong, which meant that we could spend money and find additional money. We also had a solid understanding of the building market and we certainly understood stone. We knew where the quarries were around the world. We knew what kind of stone came from each quarry. We knew how to ship it, store it and distribute it. We had relationships in place.

What we needed was a national partner who could get us into the retail sector fairly quickly and on a large enough scale to launch and build a brand. A national partner would give us the exposure we'd need right out of the gate.

Just as we were developing a plan for pitching national partners, we got a call from one such prospect. I'm not saying that figuratively. I mean that *the day after* we decided on how we would go about calling on the national partners of our choice, we got a call from one of those choices. To be even more specific, and dramatic, we got a call from our top choice. It was immediately apparent that we were both beginning a matchmaking quest for one another. Our vision seemed blessed by some business god. Our national partnership and brand seemed meant to be. Talk about vision validation!

So, as we'd done so effectively before, we began dogging the vision like people possessed. We did our homework and came up with a brand name. We made materials – signs, brochures, tags, websites – to support the brand. We sourced product and worked out distribution. We trained our partners and store associates. We created a customer service operation and network of local fabricators who would install product. It was hard, time-consuming work but work we knew how to do. At the end of the day, we'd have a national brand.

I wish that were the end of the story. I wish this were another Michael Phelps, Oprah Winfrey, Barak Obama example of how single-minded adherence to a vision pays off. But wait, there's more. So, now we had the brand; launching a brand and becoming a household name, however, are two different things. If I had known then that I would be launching a brand in an economy which was sliding fast into a recession, the depths of which have not been seen since the Great Depression, would I have really wanted to take on that challenge. My vision was not just the brand, but the longevity of the brand and the security that it represented. We were unbelievably successful, but we couldn't have seen this "economic storm" coming. Perhaps running a "little" company of 36+ employees would have been a lot more manageable *had I known then what I know now.*

Hindsight is 20/20 as they say. It's easy but only academic to look back and see what you should have done. I'm an entrepreneur, though, and entrepreneurs are driven by visions and optimism. And we always hope that with a vision and hard work, all will be well. We work like hell to meet our goals and achieve our visions. I'm going to keep doing that.

What I Wish I Knew Then That I Know Now

by Kayla Fioravanti, Chief Formulator,
Registered Aroma therapist, Essential Wholesale
www.essentialwholesale.com

If I only knew then what I know now, I would live my life exactly the same, but I wouldn't beat myself up for the chaos I create around me. I wouldn't allow others' disapproval of my creative energy to bother me. I live in a state of constant chaos with varying degrees of out-of-control pandemonium, as I balance business and family in my own unique way.

I've realized that I can't make my life fit into the world's mold - it doesn't fit. I operate well inside a world that many wouldn't enjoy. I know that is the case with most entrepreneurs. It is okay to be different. I have friends who shake their heads and say, "I don't know how you do it" but I don't know how I *wouldn't* do it. If I didn't have the things that challenge me on my plate today, I would have gathered up other challenges. It is just my nature. I find it healthiest to accept who I am and allow myself to be everything God has created me to be even if I'll never fit into a conventional mold.

I've never done anything half way or without passion. If I choose to do something it is wholeheartedly and with both feet. I've been known to jump into deep waters with my eyes closed, trusting that I not only will survive, but that I will thrive in the crisis. I tend to over-commit myself and be stretched thin. I've finally discovered that I blossom right there in the middle of the self imposed chaos. I passionately throw myself into the midst of it. And while there in the craziness of my life, instead of reaching for a life vest I grab onto more of life. Rather than drowning with my arms overflowing, I am energized and renewed by the experience.

What is balance to me is bedlam to another. There are tipping points at times that steal my laughter and at those times I fight back to reach my personal equilibrium. As the saying goes, "if mama ain't happy, ain't nobody happy." If I stop laughing and can't find humor even in the chaos, then my life is tipped out of balance, but when I am still laughing there is still hope in every situation. Along the way I have allowed myself to embrace my own sense of balance.

I am the person who will jump into a freezing river or push my body past exhaustion to reach the top of a mountain on my hands and knees just for the experience. And I am the person who will start a business on a shoestring budget. I will chase giant dreams with my husband into overwhelmingly fast paced business growth. I am the person who will fail, experience utter defeat and then jump right back into the same raging river of business. And I'm okay with that now. I'm not bothered by the people who are standing on the banks of the river shaking their heads in disapproval. I love the rush, love the experience, and I thrive in the growing and painful experiences of it all.

It was a liberating experience for me to understand that my dreams and aspirations don't have to fit into another person's vision of success. I finally realized that my family's focus on business with our children right in the middle is not wrong, just different. It isn't wrong, and it isn't right, but it is the right path for our family, even if it is different.

I also learned that it is crucial to allow yourself to blossom right where you are and stop waiting for all of your ducks to be in a row. Maybe your ducks don't fit together in a straight line. I know mine don't. The reality is that tomorrow my ducks will be scattered everywhere but when I move in one direction, they will follow me. They won't do so in an orderly fashion but my metaphoric ducks will assemble in a forward direction when I move forward. If I hang back, they hang back, and if I throw my hands up in the air and surrender, they scatter. So the very best thing I have found is to move in a forward direction towards my goals and allow my frenzied ducks to follow.

In my forties I have learned to love living out loud, with failure along with success, experiencing the strain of trials, all while walking beside my husband as we shoulder the burden together of the life we have chosen. Accepting and loving the person that I am has freed me to experience success beyond my wildest dreams. When I stopped fighting against myself I was free to succeed.

What I Wish I Knew Then That I Know Now

by Judi Sheppard Missett, Founder and CEO, Jazzercise, Inc.
www.jazzercise.com

Then I wouldn't be where I am today. I'm thankful I didn't know then what I know now because I enjoyed the journey of self discovery that led me here. I believe you know what you know at certain times in your life for a reason. This knowledge, or lack thereof, allows you to grow and keep treading forward down life's path at the right pace. To interfere with this process would undoubtedly steer you off course. I enjoyed growing organically along with my business because I had to find my own way, change and adapt in order to achieve success.

I believe in surrendering yourself to serendipity. Things have a way of coming together at the right time if you follow unexpected leads and events. There is a master plan at work and if you heed the signs, you will make the right decisions at the right moments. Be open to these opportunities that come your way and be ready to adapt to them. I always trust my gut and thus far it has never failed me. Don't be so rigid in your five or 10-year plan that you are afraid to deviate from it. Take chances. It is okay not to have a plan once in awhile. Most of my company's largest triumphs resulted from opportunities that were unplanned and unbudgeted but were simply too good to pass up.

Find your passion and pour every ounce of this passion into your business. If you don't have passion when you're building a business, then it's just going to feel like work. If you love what you do, there is no limit to the success you'll achieve. Passion enables you to do four things: fulfill your dreams, work harder than you imagined possible, listen to your instincts and accept the fact that you are different from everyone else. If being a career mom was easy, everyone would do it! Marry a man who wants to stay home. Then get out and do your thing.

As long as you follow your passion, you'll live your life with no regrets. It's okay to learn as you go and even make mistakes, but never look back. Success is not about dwelling on the past but living in the present and making plans for the future. We all grow wiser with age. I probably wouldn't have been ready to know back then what I know now. And even if I did, it probably wouldn't have made a difference.

What I Wish I Knew Then That I Know Now

by Anne Stanton, CEO, Enjoy the City
www.enjoythecity.com

There are so many similarities between running a successful business and running a successful family. Our educational system and society encourage us to focus on the tangible aspects of both, providing excellent instructions for building a solid business plan or mapping out a week's worth of healthy meals for our families, so we master those tangibles and venture out into the world to start our businesses and our families, feeling prepared and confident. We've been educated, we've studied, we've practiced in a controlled environment and now we are ready to go!

Then you open your doors for business or your heart to the love of children and you realize that there isn't a fancy business school or parenting class in the world that can fully prepare you for the "soft issues" of life. Dealing with personality conflicts, motivating and empowering people, building consensus and overcoming ego – all of these are lessons learned over time through experience.

After graduating from Harvard Business School, launching a <u>dot. com</u>, experiencing the <u>dot.com</u> crash and being forced to liquidate in a court hearing scheduled in the early morning hours of September 11, 2001, I reevaluated my life and decided it was time to move in another direction. I finally married the love of my life, five years after he'd asked my father for my hand, started a successful family business, Enjoy the City, and welcomed two wonderful children into the world. Along the way, I have learned that consistency is the key to success.

My experiences have shown if you can do the following with consistency you will be successful at home and at the office, with your children, your employees, business partners and ultimately, yourself.

- Honor your word.
- Set priorities and live your life based on those priorities.
- Uphold your values and base all of your decisions on those values.
- Take calculated risks and limit the amount of time you devote to worry.
- Own your choices and accept responsibility for them; hold others to the same standard.
- Don't be afraid of failure or the failure of others, for as Henry Ford said, "Failure is the only opportunity to begin again more intelligently."
- Take care of yourself so that you can also care for others.

If I had known, all those years ago, before grad school, before my perfect wedding in Charleston, before the miracle birth of my beautiful children, before Enjoy the City, what I know now, would I do it all again? You bet I would! I would just do it smarter, with less angst and a little more tenacity.

What I Wish I Knew Then That I Know Now

by Natalie Kennedy, Founder, Kennedy Creative
www.kennedycreative.com

I wouldn't be so hard on myself! In the beginning, you think you have to be perfect—a perfect mother, perfect business owner, perfect woman. It took me a lot of trial and error (and crying over countless cups of spilled milk) but as soon as I realized that there is no such thing as perfect, a lot of pressure was lifted off of my shoulders.

When I first started my business, I was energized, organized and optimistic. I had my Rolodex of potential clients, a tidy desk from which to conduct business and enough positive energy to quick start my cappuccino maker. Similarly, I had an intensely confident feeling when I learned I was pregnant with my first child. I read the parenting books, baby-proofed the house and was filled with anticipation and excitement about the journey that was ahead of me. I'd always been an ambitious person, and these two life changes were only going to allow me to reach my true potential…as Wonder Woman.

All it takes is one phone call from a client, one message that didn't get relayed or one sniffle from your kiddo, and your perfectly-mapped out plan is quickly changed. Out go your super-human powers and in comes reality. It's all a lesson in self-discovery. I've learned that it's okay not to have all of the answers, and that vulnerability can make you more approachable and relatable. Playing on my strengths, leaning on my support system, and being realistic about my time are all key to being able to balance my business-self, my mom-self and MYself. Given that I work in the event industry, I particularly like the phrase, "It can't all be wedding cake." To me this means that not every day can be a great day—and that's just fine by me. Wedding cake doesn't taste very good with spilled milk anyway.

What I Wish I Knew Then That I Know Now

by Julie Lenzer Kirk, President, Path Forward International
www.JulieLenzerKirk.com

It's Not Personal, It's Just Business

Let's face it, we entrepreneurs take our businesses personally. When you put your blood, sweat, and tears—and money—into something, it is hard to detach from it. What I have learned through the course of my career and with my own businesses, however, is that being able to look at our businesses objectively without taking every failure (and success) personally is crucial not only for our success, but for our sanity as well. Unfortunately, I had to learn this the hard way with customers, contracts, and employees.

Customers, Contracts, and a Handshake

When I started my first company, Applied Creative Technologies, I was fortunate to extend my relationship with a client from my corporate work to land my own first customer. There was one particular gentleman who was our main contact who also became a personal friend. He supported and encouraged my decision to leave my job for the uncertainty of self employment.

I started working with this client on an individual basis as an independent contractor. About two years into my self-employment, they had a project they wanted me to accept that would provide an opportunity to grow my business. The project was developing a production and warehousing system to replace the one I had designed for them several years earlier. They were on a tight schedule, building two new manufacturing plants, and they needed the system operational within a short amount of time. They wanted us to press ahead and didn't have time to hammer through a contract. *Trust me,* he said.

I DID trust this person; the problem was that my work wasn't just for him. It wasn't about trust, it was about setting expectations. I needed to push for a contract in spite of our relationship and perhaps even because of it. Additionally, I had been looking for an opportunity to create a product to resell to others, so I wanted to retain ownership of the software we developed. I was able to stand my ground, and we worked hard to negotiate a fair deal. Within days of signing our agreement, however, everything changed. My client was acquired by a large corporation, and I was terrified our multi-year, multi-million dollar deal would be stalled or terminated. Luckily we were far enough through the process that the new parent company gave the contract a quick review and approval, putting us on our way.

Thank goodness we took the time and trouble to get it on paper. Less than a year later, our key client contact died suddenly at the age of 48. I lost a good friend, and without a contract I could have lost a business as well. With him went a relationship that I had spent 10 years building. The personal side was gone, just like that. It was now all about business. I realized at that point the mistake I made by focusing too much of my marketing and relationship-building on one person. I had not developed advocates among his bosses or peers. While trust is important, people come and go in a business. It took a long time to build new alliances, but since that day I make sure to broaden my network within any current or prospective client.

Don't Call My Baby Ugly

Many business owners view their business as a child. I know at least one who carried around her new logo like a baby picture. *Want to see my new baby?* Another business owner publicized her website launch as a birth announcement. Some even treat their businesses better than they do their own children at times and find themselves spending more hours at work than at home. Although I certainly did not do either of those (at least not consistently), my first business was absolutely my third child. It took all my money, kept me up at night, and even sassed me back.

The problem with becoming so attached to your business is that you can lose objectivity when you get too close. I certainly got too close. I started to become defensive as customers made suggestions or pointed out issues with our software. *They must not be using it right,* I rationalized. Rather than listening with an open mind, focusing on what the customer wanted, I reacted as if they were calling my baby ugly. That immediate mother-tiger instinct welled up inside me, and I lashed out. Bad move. It upset me so much I couldn't sleep. I had to step back and look at my business and our products impartially. I had to shift the passion I felt for my business away from what we were doing to what our clients were saying. I had to focus externally on our customers' needs rather than internally on how ingenious I thought our product was. Once I did this, our business really started to soar and I started to sleep more soundly, at least for a little while.

It's All About Them

When you hire the right people into a small company, it begins to feel like a family. It didn't hurt that my first "employee" (partner, really) was my husband. With 12 people crammed into 800 square feet, we HAD to get close. I even shared an office for the first few years. We perpetuated and encouraged the collegial feel with family-focused events. We took our staff and their families to amusement parks, baseball games, laser tag and bowling. We worked hard and we played hard.

As the head of the family, I also felt the weight of the responsibility. These people left high-paying, secure jobs to come to work for a potentially-volatile start-up company - my baby. They came to work for the company because they believed in me and what we were doing. They trusted me and I returned the favor by treating them well. In fact, we instituted many policies that won us national awards for workplace excellence granting us such titles as "Great Place to Work" and "Employer of the Year."

For many years, our attrition rate was near zero. No one left who wasn't asked or whom we didn't want to leave anyway. Loyalty was high and the family remained intact. I can still remember how I felt, then, when my lead developer submitted his letter of resignation. I was crushed. *What had I done to make him want to leave?*

After talking with another employee and one of his close friends, I realized that his quitting was not about me. His decision to leave our company was difficult but he had to do what was right for himself and his family. I finally got it. It wasn't about me. It wasn't about loyalty. No matter what level of allegiance you think your employees carry for your company, at the end of the day it is all about them.

While it is important to find a business that is fed by your passion, be careful putting so much of yourself into it that you lose objectivity. When you take things too personally, you can lose your ability to make good decisions for the business, which is bad for the company and dangerous for your sanity. There needs to be some separation. While I have founded each of my subsequent businesses on passion, I've learned to keep it from becoming an obsession and taking over my life. After all, there's more to us and to life than our companies.

What I Wish I Knew Then That I Know Now

by Erika Andersen, Founder, Proteus International
www.proteusinternational.com

When I started my consulting business in 1990, my children were six and not quite two. And I didn't just begin a business, I really went in all the way: leaving a secure job, starting on a shoestring, and moving halfway across the country, from New York to Colorado, to do it. Looking back, it was a huge leap of faith. Here I was with two little kids, never having run a business, in a new town and a new part of the country, with a husband who—while supportive of my efforts—was a self-described "non-entrepreneur." And I was the primary breadwinner!

To tell the truth, if I'd known then what I know now—that most businesses fail in their first few years; that starting a business while being the mother of small children is more complicated and time-consuming than is possible to explain; that there will be months when the clients don't call back and there's little or nothing to put in the bank—I probably wouldn't have done it. So I'm really glad I *didn't* know all those things, because having my own business has been and continues to be one of most fulfilling aspects of my life: enormously challenging, consistently gratifying, even a lot of fun.

While I may not have been realistic about all the potential problems inherent in starting a business, in retrospect, I did do many other things right. First, I partnered with a knowledgeable and supportive older colleague who was able to fund our first few months of start-up. And we had both been working successfully in our field—executive coaching and consulting and management training—for years, so we had the necessary experience as well as great contacts.

Perhaps most importantly, I had an intensely clear vision of the company I wanted to create. In fact, my company's mission has remained exactly the same since the very beginning: *We help individuals and organizations clarify and move toward their hoped-for future.* I knew I wanted to build a team of really smart, authentic, insightful, flexible professionals who would be excited to help our clients get clear about the careers and businesses they wanted to create, and then help them figure out how to do just that. And now, almost 20 years later, we've built that team and it's going strong; we have wonderful clients, and they continue to call upon us over the years to help them create their future as we create ours.

What I'm saying is that it may be necessary to be a little overly optimistic when you're starting a business. Perhaps, in order to jump in with both feet, you need to have not yet discovered some of the more sobering information you'll acquire along the way. I'm not suggesting you go in with your eyes closed. Definitely do your homework, get clear about what you're trying to create and have contingency plans. Just allow your dreams to carry you beyond the statistics.

I read a wonderful quotation the other day from Colin Powell. He said, "Perpetual optimism is a force multiplier." I agree. Starting a business—especially when you're a mom, especially if your children are small—requires enormous optimism and hopefulness. And it's that very optimism that can carry you through all the obstacles ahead, to the point where your business is thriving and you feel, as I do, that every moment was worth it.

What I Wish I Knew Then That I Know Now

by Allison Gower, President, Qtags & The Platform Group

www.qtags.com

I am a lot smarter and can DO a lot more than I realized.
I started my career in marketing at large consumer products companies
with well-budgeted big brands, armed with an MBA from a top-10
business school. From day one as a professional brand manager I was
taught that there are departments that perform certain tasks, procedures
to follow, no skipping steps allowed, and, above all, there is *a right way
to do it*. This meant that I mostly attended meetings, made coffee, took
phone calls and planned travel, but did very little in the way of actually
accomplishing anything. I was busy with this approach, and because
I was occupied from early in the morning to late at night (translation,
being spotted at work before and after the executives arrived and left),
I earned promotions quickly.

When I departed the corporate world in the late '90s and set off to
make my fortune as an entrepreneur, I felt pretty confident. After all,
judging from my promotions and my success in the corporate world,
I must be pretty good at marketing. Surely success as an entrepreneur
would follow easily.

Unfortunately, the entrepreneurial success board did not get the
memo that I was a bright corporate star who should succeed because
I knew how to stay extremely busy. After a few years of long hours,
constant time at my new company's office, I had to be honest with
myself. Something was wrong; I was not close to accomplishing goals
for revenue, client relationships, networking or anything else. How
could this be? I was so busy.

And then it hit me. What I was doing was following the corporate
model of getting certain types of people to think through issues and

provide solutions, following procedures without ever skipping steps and working within accepted channels. This worked fairly well in the corporate world, where I wasn't ever really expected to affect sales or grow client relationships, but it sure wasn't getting me anywhere as an unknown president of a small, fledging company.

I adopted a new mantra—I would become my own expert. I would live my life as if I was getting a PhD in my company and its marketplace. I would learn about information technology, web-site building, advertising, art development, public relations, and social media and I would not outsource anything to anyone until I could hold an intelligent conversation about it and actually do a pretty good job of executing it myself.

Don't misunderstand me. I am not advocating that entrepreneurs do everything and never delegate or build a team. What I am suggesting is that you learn enough about any subject that has to do with your business that you can hold your own with the experts. Not only will you find that in your quest to learn about a subject, you may accidentally learn enough to do it yourself, you will also save money and time when you do hire an expert to execute because you will know what you want and have a good plan for how it should be executed. And when you build your corporate team, your staff will respect your knowledge and your ability to stay abreast of new strategies and ideas.

As an entrepreneur your time is valuable. You can choose to spend your time teaching others about your business, your ideas, and your strategies, and then hope they get it. Or you can spend your time expanding your own knowledge base. The second strategy is an investment in yourself and your company that pays huge dividends, regardless of the path you ultimately take in your business.

What I Wish I Knew Then That I Know Now

by Valerie Fitzgerald, Founder, The Valerie Fitzgerald Group
www.ValerieFitzgerald.com

I'm not ashamed to admit, I've made every mistake in the book. Between choosing partners and making business decisions, I've stumbled and fallen, yet I've always gotten back up. Despite the learning curve, I've successfully built a multi-million dollar real estate business, established a charity foundation, and continue to speak across the county to women's and business groups. All this, might I add, I accomplished while raising my daughter as a single mother. I don't think mistakes are a bad thing, and in fact, I know my mistakes got me to where I am today. That's an important lesson that isn't taught in school and is often thrown under the rug. Mistakes are simply stepping-stones to the truth of the matter, to a bigger picture, and to moving forward and achieving great things.

That being said, my success isn't completely by accident. Many years ago, I had a beautiful baby girl for whom I needed to provide. Of course that included the basic necessities, but I wanted more for this little girl. I wanted her to have every opportunity available, regardless of the fact we were a one-income household. With those things in mind, I had to make my one income big enough for all our dreams.

I didn't know the path my life would take, but I did have goals. I still set goals and take the necessary actions to achieve those goals. Knowing what you want and having a clear vision of what that is, keeps you on track for success. For as long as I can remember, I've had "vision boards." Mine have been 5x5-foot corkboards with all kinds of pictures, phrases and notes attached. Whether it was a photograph of a great vacation destination where I wanted to go, a quotation that inspired me, or an invitation to an upcoming event, my vision boards give me an outlet for getting everything out of my head and putting it in front of me, so I can see it and focus on it. Things constantly go on and off my boards, but I know that what is on the board is something into which I want to put energy and see come to fruition.

Having a clear vision, or a desired outcome, helps filter out many time consuming commitments and opportunities that don't support your vision. We are inundated daily with choices regarding how to spend our time; our money and our resources, and when we don't have a plan, the majority of us tend to deviate from our goals. When I was approached by Simon & Schuster to write my book *Heart & Sold*, it was easy to tell them, "yes." Writing a book was something I had always wanted to do, and when the opportunity presented itself, I clearly saw how the experience would align with my vision.

Regardless of the many mistakes I've made, two things are true: one, I remained focused on my goals and didn't let mistakes get in the way, and two, I never failed to recognize the lesson in the mistake. In both cases, having my goals clearly defined and in front of me, ensured I stayed on course to make my dreams come true.

What I Wish I Knew Then That I Know Now

by Dr. Elon Bomani, Founder, The Dynamic Diva
www.thedynamicdiva.com

Help, My Business and Marriage Partner Doesn't Want to be a Millionaire!

I started my road to millions by creating wealth out of necessity. My husband and I were in the midst of getting a divorce. It was on the same scale as *The War of the Roses*. We had taken our positions. He had his method of defense and I thought I had mine. Like any battle, the main focus was to win the war by any and all means necessary. He pulled out his major trump card. He emptied "our" joint checking account and transferred "our" income into another account, leaving me financially destitute. This was the epitome of emotional and financial abuse. He was the breadwinner, and I was the dependent stay-at-home mom—or so he thought. I went from being a homeless mom with $36 in my checking account to a millionaire within a year and a half of investing in real estate utilizing programs that showed me how to do it without cash or credit. It worked!

One year after accomplishing that feat, I was still married and I had built my mini real estate empire in California, where everything is community property. If I were to get a divorce, he would get half. Moreover, I would be continuing the vicious cycle of raising my son as a single mom. Growing up with a single mom on welfare and seeing how difficult it was to raise a child alone, I opted to give my marriage a second chance based on some important contingencies. My husband had to develop a wealthy conscious, become financially literate, and help me build the business.

He agreed. In the beginning of our reconciliation, he appeared quite supportive of my goals and dreams. He read the books, learned the business and helped with the child-rearing. He gave me the cooperation and encouragement I needed to get me through the daily responsibilities of running a family and a business. My son was getting the love and nurturing that every child needs during the formative years. My dream of being a successful work-at-home mom and running a successful real estate investment firm was coming true. I was on cloud nine.

Unfortunately, the second honeymoon started to fade two years into the reconciliation. My husband's interest in me, our son and the business became secondary. Begrudgingly, I became Supermom! I found myself running the business, taking care of my children and being my own support system. At the time, the real estate business was really hot, and I knew the real estate flame was going to fizzle soon. It was important for me to get the deals done before the market downturn. I was determined to succeed and prayed that the problems we had would work themselves out. I escaped into my business and raising my two boys.

Fast forward seven years after starting my wealth journey: I am happily divorced and on my new millionaire adventure with my boys in tow. Yes, I had to concede to the inevitable that my husband and business partner did not want to be a millionaire. It takes work, a lot of work, to run a family and business successfully. The same business principles of love, respect, honor, integrity, loyalty, trust and commitment are mandatory in the business of family too. We lacked all the above, and no amount of money can replace those core values.

It was never about the money or the business. I stayed married far too long because I did not want to break my sons' hearts. Divorce is not an easy road to travel with children who love both parents. Coming from a broken home, I experienced the psychological damage that I didn't want my own children to acquire. I, honestly, wanted to spare my children the hurt and pain.

In hindsight, if I had known then what I know now, I would have married someone who had the same spiritual, social and financial goals as I did. I did not ask the important questions about finances such as:

How do you feel about money? What does your financial statement look like? Do you have a budget? What is your FICO score? Women and moms who are a part of my Dynamic Diva Millionaire Mentor program must ask these questions of their mates. And, if they are not on the same accord, they must be headed in that direction or the goal of becoming a millionaire will be sabotaged. The entire family has to want to become millionaires.

If the money is "funny," there is no romance without finance. Today, the divorce statistics are staggering. The number one reason for the demise of the marriage is money problems. Moreover, the majority of the time, the woman will have to take on the full responsibility of raising the children—emotionally, physically and financially, too. So, it is paramount that women and moms who are on the journey of creating millions select a mate with the same goals in mind.

The best lessons learned are often other people's. I share my story because more than half of my wealth is now transferred to my husband. And, I am so happy for him. My peace of mind, self-worth, and well-being of my children was worth every penny. I have stated in previous speaking engagements that if I lost it all tomorrow, I was not worried because I can recoup it. You see, no one can take away the worth of education, knowledge, experience and connection that I have accumulated over the years. The first million may be the hardest, but my next millionaire adventure is going smoothly now as I write this. My kids and I will see you at the millionaire mountain top!

What I Wish I Knew Then That I Know Now

by Marsha Firestone, President & Founder,
Women Presidents' Organization
www.womenpresidentsorg.com

If I had known then what I know now, I would have been able to accomplish more of what I wanted, at an earlier age. Two of the business lessons I wish I had known are the importance of building relationships and connections with those around you—especially others in your field—and the significance money has on the work you are able to accomplish.

When I was young, I thought forming relationships and connections was based solely on performance and content. I wanted to be the best performer at everything I did, and focused more on perfection than building relationships. I realized that you can be an outstanding performer but not as successful as you might have been because you didn't take the time to build relationships. I wish I had known that putting effort into forming and developing new connections and cultivating old ones will prove to be extremely beneficial to your business.

The connections you create in your industry over time will help you and your business. Some of the first people I met when I started working are the ones I still turn to for advice. The most important business development activities are those in which you collaborate with and learn from other people. You can learn more from the interactions you have with the people around you than you can from performing highly but alone. It isn't only about making connections, but also about building and maintaining relationships, even if you do not work directly with that individual. Simple phone calls and communication will keep the relationships alive and fresh. This way, if they ever need something that you can provide, they are more inclined to turn to you first. I didn't value these important relationships until I realized how much more I could have accomplished at an earlier point in my career if I had made the effort to learn from those around me.

I was also extremely idealistic when I was younger and motivated to invest my efforts in charitable work. It wasn't until I began getting involved in such activities that I recognized the impact of money. If I had had the funds to support my endeavors, I would have been more satisfied professionally and personally with what I was doing. I ignored doing well financially and put my emphasis on achievements, realizing only later that the availability of money would have made those acts more effective.

I wish I had been more interested in attaining higher levels of financial success so that I could have supported projects to benefit women, illness, and education efforts, three of the causes about which I have always been passionate. Earlier, my feeling was that if I worked for these causes and showed how dedicated I was, the money would not matter. I know now that so much more could have been done with more resources. Now, through hard work and dedication I can support and carry out some of the charitable work I wanted to accomplish years ago. The process of learning these lessons should be available to all business owners; as with most of life it is the journey, not the destination that matters. Learning these significant lessons while building my business has helped me reach a level in my career with which I can be proud. It is not crucial to know everything when you start your business, but as long as you are open to the ideas and lessons you learn along the way, the future can be more fulfilling.

What I Wish I Knew Then that I Know Now

by Janis Spindell, Serious Matchmaking, Inc.

www.janisspindelmatchmaker.com

I started my matchmaking business back when my daughter was only six years old. At the time, I was a fashion executive and the proprietor of nine retail locations of Mommy and Me stores. Carly was my "mini-me." Everywhere I went, she went with me. I always had this uncanny knack for setting people up. For fun, I would introduce friends who I thought would be perfect for each other, and when 14 different couples I introduced all ended up getting married within one year, I knew that a matchmaker was born!

I continued to bring Carly with me everywhere, whether it was to meet potential new clients or to conduct a home visit. But once Carly entered middle school, she was at school all day and then busy with extracurricular activities all evening and could no longer accompany me.

By the time my second daughter, Falyn, came along, I was so entrenched in my business that it became too hard to bring her with me everywhere. Being an entrepreneur is the hardest thing I've ever done, but I wouldn't trade my business for anything in the world.

I wish that I had been able to spend as much time with Falyn as I had with Carly. For the first ten years of her life, Carly didn't leave my side, and now that Falyn is about to turn ten, I realize that I didn't have the same experience with her. Having my own business does allow me to leave the office to pick Falyn up at school or bring her to her after-school activities. If I had a full-time corporate job this wouldn't be possible. No matter how important my business is and always will be to me, I am first and foremost a mom, and that will never change.

What I Wish I Knew Then That I Know Now

by Cristy Clarke, Founder, Table Topics
www.tabletopics.com

How Much Cash It Takes To Grow A Business

I'd heard it was important to know your cash needs going in, and I created a basic budget, but I had not looked month-by-month at the cash going out and cash coming in. The problem is even worse if you're product is successful. I now realize, that cash is the number one thing to be concerned with at start-up.

What kept me going through all of this was that I was absolutely sure of three things: My little business idea was good for me – I needed the stimulation, challenges, the fun and excitement of building a business. It's made me a happier, more productive person. It's given me an outlet for my creativity, my business "savvy" and it expanded my appetite for risk taking. **The business was good for my family.** Our girls are growing in knowledge and self-sufficiency. I can see them approaching everything they do in a more considered, thoughtful way. They're inspired to reach out for opportunities at school, in sports, etc. I think that's a direct result of being involved in helping grow TableTopics. **My little idea was something that could really help people**—to help them lead a happier, more fulfilling life. I knew there was a need for TableTopics. I wanted to inspire fun conversations wherever they happen, knowing that it's through our conversations with our family and friends that we create lasting memories. That was my motivation to keep going despite any of the challenges or doubts I faced.

What I Wish I Knew Then That I Know Now

by Terry Wille, Executive Director for Ignite/Stream Energy
www.residualnow.info

"Eat your peas. Sit up straight. Get good grades. Be on time. Work hard. Smile and be nice." These are all useful things that I learned as a child, but I wish I had learned a few more things, "Start a business with leverage and residual income." "Implement systems so it will run without you." "Do it as soon as you can, and then go as fast as you can." "Run like your hair is on fire and don't look back."

When I started out, all I knew was to get a job and do my best. I did that, and the result of getting a job and working hard was just enough money to keep myself afloat but not enough to get ahead.

I started one business and then purchased others while raising two children. I was in charge, and I made way more money than I ever made working for somebody else. There was one problem: I didn't know how to implement systems to create leverage. My businesses owned me. I wanted my life back. It is systems and the leverage that sets a business owner free.

I sold my businesses and went back to school. I earned an NMD degree and became a Naturopathic Medical Doctor. It was a myriad of experiences—draining, exhilarating, and gratifying all at the same time. Simultaneously, I became a savvy real estate investor and later an agent. As a result, I became a millionaire mom. It was there that I got my first taste of leverage. Making money from other people's money is smarter than trading time for money, but we all know what has happened to real estate. When one door closes, another always opens!

The door that opened was one that I least expected. A coworker shared the business plan of a startup energy company that was coming to Georgia. It was network marketing. I wasn't too sure about being involved with network marketing, but there was something different about this business. It was gas and electric energy—a commodity everyone habitually used and had to pay for no matter what. To me it was a no-brainer. I followed my intuition and went for it. It was one of the best business decisions I have ever made.

Today, I am an Executive Director, one of only five in the state of Georgia. I am one of the top female money earners. I'll admit at first I did it for the money, but it is the intangibles that are the most gratifying. I'm surrounded by positive, energetic people who are investing in their lives and the lives of others. We are teaching others how to become business owners, taking advantage of leverage and proven systems to create streams of residual income. The underlying blessing is I'm changing lives for the better via this wonderful opportunity.

Network marketing is very inexpensive to start and it has all the things that business owners want: leverage, proven systems, and residual income. If I knew then what I know now, I would have looked for the best networking business and worked it as hard as I could. I would have run like my hair was on fire and not looked back! I cannot express how wonderful it is to OWN your LIFE! Go out and claim your piece of success in the world. You can do it!

What I Wish I Knew Then That I Know Now

by Kristi Frank, Founder, Saturday Morning Success Series
& Season-One Contestant on Donald Trump's 'The Apprentice'
www.SaturdayMorningSuccess.com

From Fired . . . To Tired . . . To Inspired!

It was a short distance: the journey from "You're Fired" on Season One of 'The Apprentice,' to "I'm Tired" with the unexpected (and unbelievably joyous!) birth of my son, Tyler, to "I'm Inspired" creating a new reality—my online telemarketing series, 'Saturday Morning Success' for stay-at-home moms. A short distance, perhaps, in terms of time, but a long time coming.

When I was chosen by 'The Donald' to be in the first group of women ever to appear on NBC's "The Apprentice," the excitement I felt was incomparable to anything I'd ever experienced. After all, reality guru Mark Burnett, who created "Survivor" and "The Apprentice" and many more reality hits, had reviewed over 250,000 video submissions to select eight women and eight men to take part in the premiere season of the show. So being chosen was as much of a high as being fired was a subsequent low. See, the fallacy of "reality shows" is an even harsher reality, i.e., the only person who emerges unscathed in these on-camera competitions, is the eventual winner. The rest of us are set up like proverbial bowling pins, feeling like we're truly "special" when we're chosen, then having to endure the humiliation of a network "defeat," or in my case, a nationwide firing. And the feeling that sets in post-mortem when you return home to your previous "reality" can hit like a brick, unless you have some solid footing and a strong support system.

For me, stability came in the unexpected proposal from my fiancée from before the show. And during our honeymoon, the morning sickness that revealed itself to be far more potent than the previous night's margaritas! Our son, Tyler, was born only 3 1/2 pounds, some seven weeks early, so a far more dramatic reality had entered our lives.

By the age of 25 I had earned a degree in Engineering from USC and acquired my real estate broker's license. I'd even had a few dealings in highly desirable Santa Monica real estate. But I certainly wasn't prepared for what was about to happen next.

After hearing those two dreaded words from 'The Donald' I was fortunate to take part in a whirlwind media tour, appearing as a guest on "Oprah," "The View," and "The Today Show," among others. I spoke privately with Barbara Walters and Katie Couric backstage, and on the way back home to Los Angeles began to create a business plan for my next adventure, entering the exciting world of online marketing.

I realized as I dreamed of what would make me happy in business as well as successful in life is that most women get stuck in what I sometimes call the "starter rut." It's where you have all the dreams and all the ability in the world, but you have no idea how to get started. You simply just don't know how to take that first step.

Few women mentors have been around to tell us how to get started; and the whole "working and stay-at-home-mom" issue is one of the hardest to deal with. I want to connect with other moms to encourage and guide us women through a seemingly complicated process. Sure, there are books and programs out there that can help, but with all the confusion, it's nearly impossible to know which way to turn. How did I know this? Because until I met my mentor, I was in the same position. Now I work day in and day out with women who are just like me, and I've been working hard to develop a company, easily accessible and understood, which helps women take that first step without making a crucial mistake. I motivate women for a living, which in turn motivates me and feeds my passion as well; which, in the end, is far more rewarding that being fired on national television!

Conclusion

We have traveled a long way together in this book. We've heard from dozens of incredible women who managed to grow incredibly successful businesses while raising their children (on their terms). Mom entrepreneurs—millionaires or not—remind me of the legendary dancers Fred Astaire and Ginger Rogers, both of whom were outstanding dancers. The difference, as the old saying goes, is that Ginger did it backwards and in high heels! These women tackle the world's most important job, that of "mom," and add on the pressures of running a business. Bar none, all of them have said it's been hard work, but in the end worth every moment. The women in this book have handled it with grace, and so can you!

There is no point in waiting for the future, for everything to line up perfectly. There is no guarantee of tomorrow. The perfect time is now! Build your support structure and get busy trying! Action is the hero of the day. If you take action you will get results. Once you have results you can adjust and modify until success is yours.

From my experiences having owned, operated, bought and sold thirty businesses and pieces of real estate, I am convinced that winning at the game of business takes more than being the smartest or the best educated. It's an individual's drive and commitment that counts. The person who takes action, stays focused on completing the (critical) task, and lives her life fully engaged—personally and professionally—is the true success story. These are the people truly living with zest!

To achieve your goals, be strategic, plot your course, then take action in spite of not knowing all the answers. By committing 100 percent to your business, engaging in thoughtful, high-level activity every day with a sense of urgency, you will succeed. It's only a matter of "when."

In order to accomplish anything on a grand scale, enlist people into your cause. Your enthusiasm and energy have to be contagious. Your plan has to be solid. Luck and timing help, too. As in any business, it needs to be the right idea, at the right time, with support from the right people. Start reaching out early to those who can and will help you. Share your milestones, which will ultimately make them more inclined to say "yes" if you ever need their help.

If you need or want a mentor or coach, I highly suggest you join us at www.millionairemoms.com. The community will support you in your efforts to accomplish your business and family goals. We look forward to getting to know you and hearing YOUR story.

"Success is your birthright, failure is Your Option."

Rick C. Ernst

You can email me at support@millionairemoms.com
Be sure to add me to your social networks as I truly do love hearing about your life.

Twitter: http://www.twitter.com/millionairemoms

Facebook: http://www.facebook.com/joycegrimesbone

LinkedIn: http://linkedin.com/joycebone

POWER WORD FIND!

Instructions: There were many important thoughts in this chapter. The main topics are hidden in this Power Word Find. Can you find the words in the diagram reading forwards, backwards, up, down, and diagonally? All of the words are in a straight line. Use the Power Words listed below.

C	O	M	M	U	N	I	C	A	T	I	O	N
U	A	O	F	I	R	S	Y	O	M	L	K	O
S	R	N	P	K	T	O	T	A	W	R	O	I
T	S	N	O	I	S	S	E	R	P	M	I	T
O	M	E	A	N	U	T	M	D	V	H	J	C
M	P	Y	L	A	R	Z	I	C	B	E	P	A
E	X	P	E	C	T	A	T	I	O	N	S	T
R	N	A	V	M	X	R	T	D	P	Y	A	T
C	E	S	E	T	D	O	G	K	J	L	O	O
U	T	S	R	E	A	L	I	S	T	I	C	P
S	S	I	A	N	C	E	E	T	O	M	S	P
T	I	O	G	N	I	D	N	U	F	A	P	U
O	L	N	E	S	F	I	R	G	Y	F	O	S
M		N	O	I	T	A	T	U	P	E	R	S

Power Words

Communication	Team
Opportunity	Funding
Expectations	Realistic
CANI	Passion
Impressions	Time
Action	Family
Trust	Listen
Leverage	Support
Customer	Reputation

Bonus: Health & Fitness Tips

An important part of business success is having the energy to commit to your work, day in and day out. "Whomever has the most energy wins." Enthusiasm and passion are contagious. People want to do business with passionate people who love their work. Without vitality it's hard to muster up the energy to get things done.

The body is an amazing machine. If you provide it with the basics it will serve you well. To reach your full potential give yourself the gift of exercise, nutrient dense foods, lots of water, and rest.

Here are some easy to implement tips shared by Carla Birnberg, fitness expert and founder of MizFitOnline.com.

Carla's Tips

Start taking exercise instead of coffee breaks. Did you know you can burn up to 12 calories per minute jumping rope? More if you're a fast jumper!

Try to avoid sitting for extended periods of time. To work some movement into your day, when you return phone calls pace around as you chat. This will burn calories as you work.

Floss your teeth. Studies show a correlation between longevity and regular flossing. No one is 100 percent certain yet why this is true, but sometimes the "why" doesn't matter.

Work on your balance while brushing your teeth. Stand on one foot for as long as you can without too much wobbling, then switch to the other side.

If you can't help but reach for a carbonated beverage try cutting the amount in half. Carbonation causes stomach bloating.

Make fitness a fun family event. Children model what they see. Give your family the gift of health by exercising together.

A simple way to know your meal is always at least semi-healthy is by including raw fruits and veggies every time you eat.

Remember, eating is supposed to be a pleasure. Make time to RELAX when you eat. This will aid in digestion and the absorption of nutrients.

Don't be all or nothing. It's always better to do a little than none at all. Even if you can fit only one strength training day in a week, you'll still benefit from it.

Be sure the weights you're lifting are in the ideal range. You should be tired but not in pain after 10-12 repetitions.

Walk for exercise? Be sure to bend your elbows! This action triggers your arms to move faster which, in turn, speeds up your legs!

Remember *always* to focus on your core muscles. Whether you're working at your desk or driving in the car focus on keeping the abdominal wall tight.

When stretching prior to a workout warm up for a few minutes first. This will allow your muscles to become warm and pliable.

If you have trouble sticking to an exercise program, list all the benefits you know regular exercise provides. Suggestions are: feeling healthier, sleeping better, preventing depression, and increased strength. Be sure to post this list where you'll see it as a daily reminder of the benefits of working out.

Try to take at least 20 minutes to complete a meal. This is how long it takes for your brain to recognize that your stomach is full.

Each day fill a container(s) with your daily water supply so you'll always know how much you've drunk and ensure you drink the required daily amount.

Have back up plans for all of your workouts in case life changes unexpectedly. Of course, your intention is to exercise for an hour at the gym, but what if you need to work late? Always have a Plan B ready.

Did you know in cake recipes you can switch out equal parts apple sauce to oil? You can! This will not only make the cake lighter and fluffier but will save tons of fat in the process.

**Exercises you can do at home
(using dynabands available at local retail outlets):**

For live examples of these, visit Carla at the Millionaire Moms You Tube Channel http://www.youtube.com/millionairemoms

Chest exercise: Basic push up: begin with knees bent and feet crossed at ankles. Arms are shoulder width apart and begin with arms straight/ extended. Inhale as you slowly lower down toward the floor, exhale as you push upward.

Be sure that your body is in a straight line and your core is tight as you execute move.

To ease difficulty of the exercise, begin using the wall to 'push up' against instead of the floor.

To increase difficulty, do a full push up with legs straight.

One Arm Row (back): Stand on your exercise band so that there is tension there. Exhale as you row the handle upward until arm is fully bent/at armpit level, pause briefly, inhale as you slowly lower the handle downward. Keep arm close to body as you execute movement. Focus on feeling your back muscles contract as you row upward and pause.

Bicep Curl: Stand on exercise band with feet should width apart. Hold handles with palms facing away from the body. Exhale as you curl the handles to shoulder level, pause briefly, inhale and slowly lower handles downward.

Tricep dips: Using a chair, sit down and place hands on either side of your hips. Grasp chair. Slide your rear end off the chair, supporting weight with arms. Inhale and slowly lower until your arms are bent to a 90 degree angle, exhale and straighten arms without locking out completely. As you lower your body, be sure to keep your back close to/ almost scraping the chair's edge. Too difficult? Try taking some of the weight off your arms and assist somewhat with your legs.

Too easy? Try propping your feet on a chair to place additional stress on arms.

Lateral raise (shoulders): Stand on exercise band with feet shoulder width apart. Grasp handles with arms at side and palms facing legs. Exhale and lift arms straight out to sides, pause briefly with palms facing floor, inhale and slowly lower.

Lunges: When attempting walking lunges, pay attention that your front knee does not go beyond your toes. Inhale as you lower and exhale as you move upward. Focus on the mind/muscle connection here: visualize your glutes doing the majority of the work as you lunge around house or yard.

Squats: Visualize a chair placed behind you and merely pretend to sit and rise upward. As you slowly lower down into the 'chair' focus on feeling your leg muscles work to control the speed with which you lower while fighting gravity's pull. Exhale and rise upward squeezing your glutes (a/k/a your butt) as you do so.

Plank: (core) This position is similar to the full pushup except that your weight is on your forearms and your toes. As you hold this position (for as long as you can and then take a rest period) focus on keeping your core muscles as tight as possible to stabilize your body.

Health and Fitness

ONE WORD GAME

This is your secret mission should you choose to accept it. There were a number of great tips in this chapter. To help you remember a few of them, we have selected several critical words and fashioned a game to help you think about them once again.

For this challenge, we will provide clues to help you find the word that is common to the word in the three word columns. For each line, think of a word that can be combined with all three words. For example, if you had "water," "baby" and "neck," the common word would be "bottle."

- Water **bottle**
- Baby **bottle**

Bottleneck whale *Instructions: For this challenge, look at the puzzle below. For each row there are three words. Use the partial word in the clue column to think of a word that can be combined with all three words (word 1, word 2, word 3). To help you we provided a few letters of each of the clue words. We also provided dashes to represent the number of missing letters in each clue word. Good luck! This is a tough one!*

Clue	Word 1	Word 2	Word 3
BR _ _ K	coffee	dance	neck
C_ R _	hard	en	apple
M_ _ L	corn	bone	oat
S_ _	baby	ups	out

Still having trouble? This excerpt from the Health and Fitness chapter may provide helpful hints for the puzzle. Read it to see if it helps you discover the missing words. **Health & Fitness Tips**

Even when working, try to avoid sitting for extended periods of time. Do you have lots of calls to return? Use that time to pace as you chat and even burn calories while you work. Start taking exercise breaks not coffee breaks! Did you know you can burn up to 12 calories per minute jumping rope? More if you're a fast jumper! A simple way to know your meal is always at least semi-healthy is by including raw fruits or veggies every time you eat. Remember, eating is supposed to be a pleasure. Make time to RELAX when you eat. This will aid in digestion and the absorption of nutrients. Remember to *always* focus on your core muscles. Whether you're working at your desk or driving in the car, focus on keeping the abdominal wall tight. Try to take at least 20 minutes to complete a meal. This is how long it takes for your brain to recognize that your stomach is full.

Answer Pages

Chapter 1 Word Bank Puzzle

Mental image	**Vision**	provides	clarity
Lucidity	**Clarity**	provides	confidence
Deed	Sureness	spurs	**action**
Victory	Action	spurs	**success**

Vision provides clarity
Clarity provides confidence
Sureness spurs action
Action spurs success

www.millionairemoms.com

Chapter 3 Overcoming Fear

ONE WORD GAME

That's where the fruit is.

T	H	A	T		I	S		
W	H	E	R	E		T	H	E
F	R	U	I	T		I	S	

Next time you are worried about taking a risk, remember:
"Don't be afraid to go out on a limb. That's where the fruit is."

-H. Jackson Browne, Jr., American author

Chapter 4 Time Management

BEFORE AND AFTER GAME

FIT Profit

Fitness

Bene**fit Focus** – think binocular

Immediate – think clock, think now

To Do – think note pad

If you are still not sure if you will be able to remember this saying.

Then Try this: *Photocopy the image, print it, and cut it out and then carry in your pocket!*

Chapter 5 Business Advice

POWER WORD FIND!

C	O	M	M	U	N	I	C	A	T	I	O	N
U								M				O
S					T			A				I
T	S	N	O	I	S	S	E	R	P	M	I	T
O				N	U	T	M					C
M			L	A	R		I					A
E	X	P	E	C	T	A	T	I	O	N	S	T
R	N	A	V							Y		T
	E	S	E							L		O
	T	S	R	E	A	L	I	S	T	I	C	P
	S	I	A							M		P
	I	O	G	N	I	D	N	U	F	A		U
	L	N	E							F		S
		N	O	I	T	A	T	U	P	E	R	

Power Words

Communication	Leverage	Family
Expectations	Customer	Listen
CANI	Funding	Support
Impressions	Realistic	Reputation
Action	Passion	Team
Trust	Time	

Chapter 5 Health & Fitness

ONE WORD GAME

Break (take exercise breaks)	1	Coffee	Dance	Neck
Core (exercise your core)	2	hard	en	apple
Meal (eat healthy meals)	3	Corn	bone	oat
Sit (avoid long periods – pace and chat)	4	baby	ups	out

Next Steps:
So What Do I Do Now?

Congrats on sticking with it this long. Most people quit but not you! So now what? You have the desire but you need more. By now you should know that talk is cheap and action is where it is at. Start implementing the principles you learned within the context of the book. You have the concepts, now it's time to start applying them to *your* life. What follows are a number of ways we can continue to work together if you need a helping hand.

Tony Robbins says, "Never leave the scene of a goal without taking an action towards its accomplishment." That's declaring your commitment.

I invite you to take the first step *right now* towards financial freedom and creating your ideal life by surrounding yourself with like-minded people. Stop reading, go to <u>www.millionairemoms.com</u> and sign up. By becoming a member you are taking a big step towards making your dream a reality! Congratulations on taking the first step towards your ideal life. You deserve it! It is here that you can start asking questions and getting feedback, not only from me but from the other members. **Be sure to sign up for the complimentary eZine on the site as well** to be inspired by a different millionaire mom's story each week.

Book Bonus:

Bonus offer: provide proof of Purchase and receive free admission into any one hour Millionaire Mom teleseminar delivered by Joyce, of your choice.

Home Learning Programs

Visit the millionairemoms.com store for home-learning programs. There is a home study course for every key driver in business (marketing, sales, operations, inventors, internet marketing, social networking, multi-level marketing, real estate, retail, franchises, manufacturing, etc) from Joyce and her top-level experts. For full details go to www. millionairemoms.com Store. We can be contacted directly at support@ millionairemoms.com or call 1-888-310-1485.

Coaching

What is more powerful than having a coach holding you accountable and guiding you each week? Put your business and personal growth on steroids by being coached to success! We have proven programs in place to get you where you want to go in a hurry. Call us to discuss packages customized to suit your individual needs 1-888-310-1485.

Seminars

If you prefer to learn in person, you may want to attend our monthly live events and mastermind groups, designed to help each woman at her particular stage: beginners, active business owners and millionaire moms. Please contact us for dates and times. Visit the website or call 1-888-310-1485 for more information.

Millionaire Mom's Getaway Weekends

Are you ready to immerse yourself in the ultimate mastermind group experience? Prepare for the most fun you've ever had! You will be surrounded by successful, entrepreneurial women ready to explore, learn and have fun! This is not your typical mastermind group. We meet in beautiful locations and participate in daily adventures, all the while networking and sharing best practices. Or, if you just need a break, chill out and relax at the spa! It's a super fun weekend.

Sometimes stepping back and allowing some breathing room affords the opportunity to see what is working and what isn't. Be personally mentored by millionaire moms and gift yourself with the opportunity to recharge. Contact support@millionairemoms.com for more information.

Speaking Engagements

Joyce Bone is a dynamic speaker who delivers her message with passion! Her presentations convey the perfect blend of street-smart success strategies with enlightened wisdom from someone who has "been there, done that." She uses humor and fun to help the audience get their "aha" moments from every talk she delivers. Her timeless lessons will leave audiences feeling ready to take on the world!

Have Joyce Bone speak at your next convention or meeting and "Wow" your group! Visit her website at
www.millionairemoms.com
for information about her speaking engagements or email
support@millionairemoms.com.
Her office can be reached at 1-888-310-1485.

AUTHOR'S NOTE

It is my hope you will consider volunteering for or contributing financially to a non-profit in your community. Be an agent of change. You will live a more rewarding life as a result and those in need will be blessed.

I've listed my favorite non-profits below, each of which is making a dramatic difference in our world through their service. A portion of the proceeds from the sale of this book and all sales made within the Millionaire Moms.com organization is donated to these organizations.

Camp Better America
www.campbetteramerica.com
888-310-1485 or kimsburleson@yahoo.com.

Camp Better America is on a mission to reconnect and support military families, giving them the tools they need to create, build and achieve their dreams. After a lengthy separation many military families experience difficulty readjusting and establishing the new "norm" at home and work.

Camp Better America helps by equipping these families with the knowledge and support they need to successful start the next chapter of their lives. A dream team of celebrities, business experts, financial experts, corporate sponsors, sports legends, chefs and every day people contribute their time and money to serving those who were willing to pay the ultimate price for our freedom. Military servicemen and women are vital to the spine of America. The camp affords all American's the opportunity to return the salute by serving these soldiers and their families.

Please visit our website at www.campbetteramerica.com to help us return the salute.

American Cancer Society
www.cancer.org
1-800-ACS-2345
The American Cancer Society is the nationwide, community-based, voluntary health organization dedicated to eliminating cancer as a major health problem by preventing cancer, saving lives, and diminishing suffering from cancer, through research, education, advocacy, and service.

American Diabetes Association
www.diabetes.org
1-800-DIABETES (1-800-342-2383)
There are nearly 24 million children and adults in the U.S. with diabetes. The American Diabetes Association is leading the fight against the deadly consequences of diabetes and fighting for those affected by diabetes. The Association funds research to prevent, cure, and manage diabetes; delivers services to hundreds of communities; provides objective and credible information; and gives voice to those denied their rights because of diabetes. Their mission is prevent and cure diabetes and to improve the lives of all people affected by diabetes.

National Kidney Foundation
www.kidney.org
1-800-622-9010
The National Kidney Foundation, a major voluntary nonprofit health organization, is dedicated to preventing kidney and urinary tract diseases, improving the health and well-being of individuals and families affected by kidney disease and increasing the availability of all organs for transplantation. NKF provides patient and community services, conducts extensive public and professional education, advocates for patients through legislative action and supports kidney research.

YMCA

www.YMCA.net

(800) 872-9622

The 2,686 YMCAs across the country build strong kids, strong families, and strong communities. Their mission is to put Christian principles into practice through programs that build healthy spirit, mind, and body for all.

JA Worldwide ™ (Junior Achievement)

www.ja.org

(719)540-8000

JA Worldwide is a partnership between the business community, educators and volunteers, all working together to inspire young people to dream big and reach their potential. JA's hands- on, experiential programs teach the key concepts of work readiness, entrepreneurship and financial literacy to young people all over the world.

We specialize in eLearning,
Games and simulations are
the ideal way to help
people learn information
quickly and retain it.
We work with your experts
to turn your content into
intriguing interactive events.

sillymonkey@mindspring.com

404.966.2372

www.sillymonkeyinternational.com

BUY A SHARE OF THE FUTURE IN YOUR COMMUNITY

These certificates make great holiday, graduation and birthday gifts that can be personalized with the recipient's name. The cost of one S.H.A.R.E. or one square foot is $54.17. The personalized certificate is suitable for framing and will state the number of shares purchased and the amount of each share, as well as the recipient's name. The home that you participate in "building" will last for many years and will continue to grow in value.

Here is a sample SHARE certificate:

HABITAT FOR HUMANITY

THIS CERTIFIES THAT

__YOUR NAME HERE__

HAS INVESTED IN A HOME FOR A DESERVING FAMILY

1985-2005

TWENTY YEARS OF BUILDING FUTURES IN OUR COMMUNITY ONE HOME AT A TIME

1200 SQUARE FOOT HOUSE @ $65,000 = $54.17 PER SQUARE FOOT
This certificate represents a tax deductible donation. It has no cash value.

YES, I WOULD LIKE TO HELP!

I support the work that Habitat for Humanity does and I want to be part of the excitement! As a donor, I will receive periodic updates on your construction activities but, more importantly, I know my gift will help a family in our community realize the dream of homeownership. **I would like to SHARE in your efforts against substandard housing in my community!** *(Please print below)*

PLEASE SEND ME _____ SHARES at $54.17 EACH = $ $_____

In Honor Of: _____

Occasion: (Circle One)   HOLIDAY   BIRTHDAY   ANNIVERSARY

       OTHER: _____

Address of Recipient: _____

Gift From: _____ *Donor Address:* _____

Donor Email: _____

I AM ENCLOSING A CHECK FOR $ $_____ **PAYABLE TO HABITAT FOR HUMANITY** <u>OR</u> **PLEASE CHARGE MY VISA OR MASTERCARD** *(CIRCLE ONE)*

Card Number _____ Expiration Date: _____

Name as it appears on Credit Card _____ Charge Amount $ _____

Signature _____

Billing Address _____

Telephone # Day _____ Eve _____

PLEASE NOTE: Your contribution is tax-deductible to the fullest extent allowed by law.
Habitat for Humanity • P.O. Box 1443 • Newport News, VA 23601 • 757-596-5553
www.HelpHabitatforHumanity.org